JAMES PATTERSON

Courtesy of Sue Solie Patterson.

JAMES PATTERSON

A Critical Companion

Joan G. Kotker

CRITICAL COMPANIONS TO POPULAR CONTEMPORARY WRITERS
Kathleen Gregory Klein, Series Editor

Greenwood Press
Westport, Connecticut • London

Library of Congress Cataloging-in-Publication Data

Kotker, Joan G.
James Patterson : a critical companion / Joan G. Kotker.
p. cm.—(Critical companions to popular contemporary writers, ISSN 1082–4979)
Includes bibliographical references and index.
ISBN 0–313–32085–3
1. Patterson, James, 1947—Criticism and interpretation. 2. Detective and mystery stories, American—History and criticism. 3. African American police in literature. 4. Cross, Alex (Fictitious character). 5. Washington (D.C.)—In literature. I. Title. II. Series.
PS3566.A822Z75 2004
813′.54—dc22 2003026654

British Library Cataloguing in Publication Data is available.

Library of Congress Catalog Card Number: 2003026654
ISBN: 0–313–32085–3
ISSN: 1082–4979

First published in 2004

Greenwood Press, 88 Post Road West, Westport, CT 06881
An imprint of Greenwood Publishing Group, Inc.
www.greenwood.com

Printed in the United States of America

The paper used in this book complies with the Permanent Paper Standard issued by the National Information Standards Organization (Z39.48–1984).

10 9 8 7 6 5 4 3 2 1

Contents

Series Foreword

The authors who appear in the series Critical Companions to Popular Contemporary Writers are all best-selling writers. They do not simply have one successful novel, but a string of them. Fans, critics, and specialist readers eagerly anticipate their next book. For some, high cash advances and breakthrough sales figures are automatic; movie deals often follow. Some writers become household names, recognized by almost everyone.

But, their novels are read one by one. Each reader chooses to start and, more importantly, to finish a book because of what she or he finds there. The real test of a novel is in the satisfaction its readers experience. This series acknowledges the extraordinary involvement of readers and writers in creating a best-seller.

The authors included in this series were chosen by an Advisory Board composed of high school English teachers and high school and public librarians. They ranked a list of best-selling writers according to their popularity among different groups of readers. For the first series, writers in the top-ranked group who had received no book-length, academic, literary analysis (or none in at least the past 10 years) were chosen. Because of this selection method, Critical Companions to Popular Contemporary Writers meets a need that is being addressed nowhere else. The success of these volumes as reported by reviewers, librarians, and teachers led to an expansion of the series mandate to include some writers with wide critical attention—Toni Morrison, John Irving, and Maya Angelou, for example—to extend the usefulness of the series.

The volumes in the series are written by scholars with particular expertise in analyzing popular fiction. These specialists add an academic focus to the popular success that these writers already enjoy.

The series is designed to appeal to a wide range of readers. The general reading public will find explanations for the appeal of these well-known writers. Fans will find biographical and fictional questions answered. Students will find literary analysis, discussions of fictional genres, carefully organized introductions to new ways of reading the novels, and bibliographies for additional research. Whether browsing through the book for pleasure or using it for an assignment, readers will find that the most recent novels of the authors are included.

Each volume begins with a biographical chapter drawing on published information, autobiographies or memoirs, prior interviews, and, in some cases, interviews given especially for this series. A chapter on literary history and genres describes how the author's work fits into a larger literary context. The following chapters analyze the writer's most important, most popular, and most recent novels in detail. Each chapter focuses on one or more novels. This approach, suggested by the Advisory Board as the most useful to student research, allows for an in-depth analysis of the writer's fiction. Close and careful readings with numerous examples show readers exactly how the novels work. These chapters are organized around three central elements: plot development (how the story line moves forward), character development (what the reader knows of the important figures), and theme (the significant ideas of the novel). Chapters may also include sections on generic conventions (how the novel is similar or different from others in its same category of science fiction, fantasy, thriller, etc.), narrative point of view (who tells the story and how), symbols and literary language, and historical or social context. Each chapter ends with an "alternative reading" of the novel. The volume concludes with a primary and secondary bibliography, including reviews.

The alternative readings are a unique feature of this series. By demonstrating a particular way of reading each novel, they provide a clear example of how a specific perspective can reveal important aspects of the book. In the alternative reading sections, one contemporary literary theory—way of reading, such as feminist criticism, Marxism, new historicism, deconstruction, or Jungian psychological critique—is defined in brief, easily comprehensible language. That definition is then applied to the novel to highlight specific features that might go unnoticed or be understood differently in a more general reading. Each volume defines two or three specific theories, making them part of the reader's understanding of how diverse meanings may be constructed from a single novel.

Taken collectively, the volumes in the Critical Companions to Popular Contemporary Writers series provide a wide-ranging investigation of the complexities of current best-selling fiction. By treating these novels seriously as both literary works and publishing successes, the series demonstrates the potential of popular literature in contemporary culture.

Kathleen Gregory Klein
Southern Connecticut State University

1

The Life of James Patterson

FAMILY BACKGROUND AND EDUCATION

James B. Patterson was born March 22, 1947, in Newburgh, New York, the only son of Charles and Isabelle Patterson. His mother was a teacher and his father an insurance executive. Three sisters followed Patterson, bringing the family to six. His grandparents also lived in the town, where they ran a small restaurant. Their cook was African American and, in an interview, Patterson tells Lewis Burke Frumkes that,

> At one point, when I was about 2 or 3, she was having trouble with her husband. . . . She moved into our house and lived with us for about four years. She and I became unbelievably close. I spent incredible amounts of time with her and her family—aunts, uncles, nephews. She eventually went back to Detroit, where she was from. . . . That was very hard for me. . . . That's where my notion of the Cross family comes from. It comes from her family. (2000, 13)

It seems likely that Patterson has conflated both his own mother and this cook into not only Nana Mama, a continuing character in the Cross novels who is a teacher as well as an African American, but also into Jimmy Horn's mother in *The Thomas Berryman Number,* also an African American teacher. Both women are affectionately drawn as wise, compassionate people, and to the extent that they reflect their real-life models, Patterson has paid loving tribute to them.

It is also possible that Patterson has used his three sisters as models for the relationship between his four women detectives (one professional, three specialized amateurs) who appear in his most recent works, the Women's Murder Club series. These women relate with warmth and humor to each other, and rely on one other for support and guidance. Their interactions feel true to life, and Patterson's sisters would indeed be fortunate if he is reflecting something of their relationships with one another here.

In addition to this family background, Patterson also has clearly used his personal traumas as elements in his stories, in particular, the death of Jane Blanchard, his long-time companion. Over and over again, there is a strong element of loss in his novels, beginning with the drive-by shooting of Alex Cross's wife in the first of the Cross series, *Along Came a Spider*.

BEGINNINGS AS A WRITER

Unlike most children who grow up to be writers, Patterson was not a compulsive reader when he was young, nor does he report the need to escape into fiction and fantasy, as so many aspiring writers have done. Instead, he came from a balanced, loving home and when he looks back on himself as an adolescent, he describes himself as a "reluctant reader," something he attributes to teaching that "crushed the life out of books" (Bernard and Zaleski 1996, 58). However, in the summer of his freshman year in college he worked as an aide at McLean Hospital, a mental institution that was at that time one of the best in the country, if not *the* best. The poet Robert Lowell was a patient there, and he used to read to the other patients and the aides. Patterson says that Lowell "couldn't go out of the hall unescorted, so he'd say, 'Hey, Jimmy, wanna go for a walk?' . . . When he was not depressed, he would talk about his poems and why he wrote them" (Speidel 1995, 83). From this Patterson's love of reading began and he himself started writing, although he is very reticent about his early work. He majored in English at Manhattan College and then earned a Master of Arts at Vanderbilt, where he became "the first Vanderbilt student since James Dickey to submit fiction . . . for a master's in English" (Bernard and Zaleski 1996, 58). The resulting novel, *Father Wrote a Hemingway Novel*, has never been published, although, given Patterson's enormous popularity, it seems more than likely that at some point it will be, if only to satisfy his readers' curiosity about his literary beginnings.

Two works that have been instrumental in determining the tack Patterson subsequently took as a writer are the novels *The Exorcist* (Blatty 1971) and *The Day of the Jackal* (Forsyth 1971). These were his introduction to popular fiction and he decided there and then that he wanted to do this type of writing, stories that would be based on suspense and excitement. Even so, he was still looking at writing as a sideline. "I never thought of making it as a writer," he told Bernard and Zaleski. "That seemed presumptuous to me" (1996, 58). Instead he went to work as a junior copyeditor for the J. Walter Thompson advertising agency, one of the most successful agencies in the country, and continued to write on the side. His career at the agency was meteoric, in part because of his throwing himself into the work after the death of Blanchard; from his beginnings as copyeditor he went on to become CEO, then Chairman, and then Worldwide Creative Director. Patterson says that he enjoyed his time in advertising, telling Speidel, "I like to go inside myself, but I also need to go outside and meet other people, and I like the ad work" (1995, 83). He made good use of the expertise gained in that world by directing the advertising campaign for his initial Alex Cross novel, *Along Came a Spider.* "Publishers haven't had a very good experience with advertising," he told John R. Hayes. "They tend to spread the money all over and do look-alike ads nobody notices. A book is like any other new product. You've got to let people know it's there and what it is. If you don't do that, don't blame the product" (1993, 128).

The result of Patterson's work was that *Along Came a Spider* became his first best-seller, and since then he has taken a lead role in the marketing of all his novels. His publishers credit Patterson's superb marketing sense with the phenomenal success his books have achieved, earning him, according to *Forbes,* $50 million a year and tying him with Stephen King as the top-grossing novelist of all time (Kellner 2002, 112). Even though Patterson is now formally retired from J. Walter Thompson, he is still both writer and publicist, a combination that so far is working very well for him.

In terms of his writing schedule, Patterson says that he writes every day and that he tries to do it in the mornings, since that was his schedule when he was in advertising. He also says that he uses outlines: "If you want to write a novel where plot is important, you must outline it first or you will waste an incredible amount of time and energy" (Frumke 2000, 13). This is certainly true of his first published novel, *The Thomas Berryman Number,* which by my count has a grand total of 43 shifts in place or time. When I was writing about the novel, I found that I had to do an outline just to track these shifts; Patterson's filling in the background for each must have been an exercise worthy of a chess master, and the novel is clearly the work of a writer who loves to plan as much as he loves to write.

DEVELOPMENT AS A WRITER

While Patterson is best known as the author of the Alex Cross novels, he has written fiction in a variety of genres: amateur detective novel, police procedural, thriller, science fiction, romance, sports, and the historical novel. In the area of non-fiction, Patterson has, with his J. Walter Thompson co-worker Peter Kim, written two books best described as sociological works: *The Day America Told the Truth* (1991), a national survey of people's attitudes toward various topics and social issues, and *The Second American Revolution* (1994), which identifies a number of social problems and adopts a town meeting framework to discuss and resolve them.

Patterson's first published novel was the Edgar-award winning amateur detective novel, *The Thomas Berryman Number* (1976), and many of his subsequent themes can be seen in nascent form here: the African American family as a role model for all races to aspire to, the sociopathic killer, the use of setting to authenticate character, and the convention of short, location-shifting chapters to keep the reader alert to what will come next. *The Thomas Berryman Number* was followed by the thrillers *Season of the Machete* (1977), a novel that extends what Thomas Berryman and his lover Oona Quinn may have become, had Berryman lived, and *See How They Run* (1979), which introduces what will be an on-going theme in Patterson novels, the irrevocable pain of loss. His next work was quite different; it is the contemporary science fiction novel *Virgin* (1980), which examines the possible result of a Biblical prophecy coming true. *Virgin* was followed by two more thrillers, *Black Market* (1986) and *The Midnight Club* (1989), at which point, with the publication of the first Alex Cross novel, *Along Came a Spider* (1993), Patterson hit his stride as a best-selling writer and as the creator of the beloved series characters, Alex Cross, Cross's family, and Cross's police partner, John Sampson. *Along Came a Spider* was followed by *Kiss the Girls* (1995), *Jack & Jill* (1996), the non-Cross thriller *Hide and Seek* (1996), a delightful fairy tale of a sports novel, *Miracle on the 17th Green*, written with Peter de Jonge (1996), and then Patterson returned to Alex Cross with 1997's *Cat & Mouse*. After the publication of *Cat & Mouse* Patterson shifted to yet another genre of popular fiction with *When the Wind Blows* (1998), a work of speculative science fiction that looks at possible outcomes of bio-genetic engineering. The next year he returned to the Cross series with *Pop! Goes the Weasel* (1999) and followed it with *Roses Are Red* (2000), *Violets Are Blue* (2001), and *Four Blind Mice* (2002), bringing the total number of Cross books to eight, as of this writing. (All are covered in this Critical Companion.)

In 2001 Patterson published the first work in what promises to be an on-going new series, the novel *1st to Die*. This series successfully combines the police procedural with the amateur detective novel, featuring a police detective, a crime reporter, an assistant district attorney, and a medical examiner, all of whom work together to solve murders. *1st to Die* was followed by *2nd Chance* (2002), written with Andrew Gross and utilizing the same group of characters. (This series is also covered in this Critical Companion.) In 2001 Patterson also published his first romance novel, *Suzanne's Diary for Nicholas,* and in 2002, an amateur-sleuth murder mystery, *The Beach House,* co-written with de Jonge. Patterson then returned to speculative science fiction with 2003's *The Lake House,* a sequel to *When the Wind Blows.* Finally, Patterson's most recent novel is 2003's *The Jester,* his first foray into the world of the historical novel; again, it is co-authored with Andrew Gross.

GOALS

First and foremost, Patterson is a storyteller. He has said, "When people think of my books, I want them to say, 'I can't put those down'" (Speidel 1995, 83). In an interview on iVillage.com he advises young writers, "Stop trying to write sentences and start trying to write stories. Stories are easy to write because they flow out of our brains naturally; sentences are extremely hard." Patterson has expanded on this, telling Bernard and Zalenski that over time his writing has evolved and has moved from emphasis on the writing itself to emphasis on the story, saying, "At this point, I'm much heavier into the telling of the story, and a little less careful with the writing of good sentences" (1996, 58). Of course, this may simply reflect the fact that given his extensive writing experience, and building on two degrees in English, Patterson no longer needs to focus on the craft of writing to the extent that he had to when he began, that much of the craft is now second nature. Certainly, even his earliest work shows more emphasis on plot than character, always the sign of an author who is interested above all in the tale rather than in the telling, and the later works read very smoothly—there is no sense here that technique has been sacrificed to story line. Thus, the evolution that Patterson sees in his work may well be more apparent to him than to his readers.

CHRONOLOGY OF EVENTS

1947	March 22: James B. Patterson born to Isabelle Morris Patterson and Charles Patterson
1969	Graduated from Manhattan College, BA, English major, Phi Beta Kappa
1970	Graduated from Vanderbilt University, MA in English
1971	Joins J. Walter Thompson Co., junior copywriter
1976	President and Associate Creative Supervisor, J. Walter Thompson
1976	Publication of first novel, *The Thomas Berryman Number*
1977	Awarded Mystery Writers of America Award for Best First Novel, *The Thomas Berryman Number*
1981	Companion Jane Blanchard diagnosed with brain tumor
1984	Death of Jane Blanchard
1988	CEO, J. Walter Thompson
1989	Worldwide Creative Director, J. Walter Thompson
1993	Publication of *Along Came a Spider,* first Alex Cross novel and first best-seller
1997	Marriage to Sue Solie
1998	Birth of son, Jack
2001	Publication of first Women's Murder Club novel

2

Genre

OVERVIEW

Holman and Harmon define genre as a device "used to designate the types or categories into which literary works are grouped according to form, technique, or sometimes, subject matter" (1992, 212). Classic literary genres include the novel, the short story, poetry, drama, and the like. Within each of these genres there are further subgenres, such as, in the category of novels, the science fiction novel, the mystery novel, the romance novel, the espionage novel, and so on. Holman and Harmon note that genre boundaries "have been much subject to flux and blur in recent times, and it is almost the rule that a successful work will combine genres," a statement that is certainly true of James Patterson's novels, where a single work might combine the mystery sub-genre known as the police procedural, the romance, the gothic genre, horror, and the sociological novel (*Along Came a Spider*, discussed in Chapter 4, is an excellent example of such cross-genre writing).

Another way of classifying literature, particularly among American academic critics, is to break it into two broad categories, that of popular fiction and that of mainstream fiction. The primary distinctions between the two are the demands they place on the reader and consequently the audiences they are intended for. As is obvious from the term "popular fiction," this is a class of fiction intended for a mass audience, one that is designed to meet the already-established expectations of a particular group. Patterson readers expect to open one of his books to a fast-paced literary world in which they constantly have to second-guess seemingly obvious solutions that then turn out to be not so obvious after all, indeed, that turn out to be incorrect, and Patterson makes a point of fulfilling these expectations. Another distinguishing characteristic between the two types of literature is the overall world view presented in each. In these terms, popular fiction is a comforting fiction in that it seldom challenges the reader's preconceptions of how the world works: ultimately, in this fiction, the guilty are identified and punished, the innocent are vindicated, our questions are answered, and we are assured that the world is both knowable and predictable. Readers leave these stories entertained and unchallenged in their basic conceptions.

In contrast, mainstream fiction has no clearly defined audience with clearly defined expectations. Instead, it must create its own audience, made up of readers who agree, before even opening a book, to question their preconceptions and who look forward to having their views challenged by the fictional world they enter. They must be active readers, willing to participate in the story with the author by taking an active role in working out its meaning, and they must also be willing to tolerate a work in which, ultimately, the guilty may never be known or may escape all punishment, and the questions raised by a given work may remain unanswered. An underlying message of virtually all popular literature is that if one perseveres, things will work out; an underlying message of virtually all mainstream literature is that we have no choice but to persevere in the face of the fact that things may never work out.

While mainstream fiction is without doubt the more difficult of these two fictions because of the demands it places on the reader, popular fiction also has much to recommend it: it is no small thing to be entertained, to escape one's immediate world for an imaginary world, and ultimately to be returned safely and without challenge to the place where we started out, and this is the promise that all good popular fiction delivers on in an unstated pact with its readers. All of Patterson's fiction falls into the area of popular literature, and he writes in many different genres, both as a single author and as a co-author: romance, fantasy, the historical novel, and even a sports novel. It is as though he thoroughly enjoys writing entertaining fiction, so much so that he gets great pleasure in trying his hand at the different sub-genres of that class. Over and over again, though, he returns to the mystery, and it is here that he is best known, both because of his first, Edgar Award–winning novel, *The Thomas Berryman Number*, and because of the success of his eight-novel Alex Cross series, and because of the promise of his new Women's Murder Club series.

MYSTERY

The mystery genre, as such, is by general agreement considered to be an American invention, with the first of the type being Edgar Allan Poe's "The Murders in the Rue Morgue" (1841). While the form has now become virtually universal, all mysteries share certain basic conventions: a serious crime, usually murder, is committed; a detective who may be either an amateur or a member of the police is brought in to investigate the crime; the focus of the story then shifts to the gathering of clues and collecting of information, and, when this is completed, the solution to the crime is announced; finally, the fate of the criminal is resolved in some manner, either through death, imprisonment, suicide, or rarely, by the criminal escaping. There are any number of variations that can be played on this basic model, one of them being the police procedural, a form that Patterson uses in all the novels covered here with the exception of *The Thomas Berryman Number,* which is a classic mystery following the pattern outlined above. The remainder of the novels, the Alex Cross and the Women's Murder Club books, all make use of the procedural format. In this sub-genre, the focus is on a group of professional detectives who, as members of a police force, investigate crimes for a living rather than as an interesting hobby. The emphasis of their work is reliance on standard police procedures to solve crimes rather than on the brilliant insights and intuitions of larger-than-life genius detectives such as Sherlock Holmes and Nero Wolfe. There is also greater realism in this sub-genre, with its references to the difficulties of the job: low pay and long hours, and the stresses these conditions place on the home life of the detectives. They usually include the spouses and children of the police with, often, a plot strand that discusses the guilt that goes along with the job because of the often-necessary neglect of family. Finally, as noted in *The Guide to United States Popular Culture,* the overriding characteristic of police procedurals is their positive image of the police: "Neither bumpkins nor geniuses, cops are drawn as honest, hardworking professionals who do difficult, dangerous, and often thankless jobs" (Kotker 2001, 618).

A second variation on the mystery that Patterson makes use of is the sub-genre of true crime. As the term indicates, this is the re-telling of crimes that have actually occurred. Anderson-Boerger, writing in *The Oxford Companion to Crime and Mystery Writing,* notes that the sub-genre is considered by many critics to pre-date the mystery genre itself, perhaps dating back to Daniel Defoe's 1725 publication of *A True and Genuine Account of the Life and Actions of the Late Jonathan Wild.* Two ways in which this sub-genre differs from mystery and detective fiction as a whole are that the outcome is known at the very beginning, and, as Mary Jean DeMarr notes, "Most accounts contain an extensive report on the trial of the culprit, the point before which mystery novels usually conclude" (2001, 857). Anderson-Boerger believes that true crime is actually more compelling than fictional crime, since "Truth is stranger than fiction and, therefore, more shocking" (1999, 469). Certainly, mystery and detective writers have a long history of utilizing true crime in their fiction: Edgar Allan Poe (1809–1849), Wilkie Collins (1824–1889), Dorothy L. Sayers (1893–1957), and Raymond Chandler (1888–1959) have all based works on actual crimes. James Patterson makes extensive use of this sub-genre in *The Thomas Berryman Number,* a novel with repeated references to the assassinations of John F. Kennedy, Martin Luther King, and Medgar Evers, and in *Along Came a Spider,* a novel based on child kidnappings, which refers back to the 1932 kidnapping of the Lindbergh baby.

POPULAR ROMANCE

Another common strand in James Patterson's work is the use of a romantic plot as a secondary element. These plots appear in 9 of the 10 procedurals covered in this companion, with only *Pop! Goes the Weasel* lacking such a component. Rosenberg and Herald define the basic theme of the popular romance as "true love triumphant against all odds" (1991, 143) but in the hands of Patterson, the formula is often inverted and could better be described as "true love defeated," as it is in *Along Came a Spider, Roses Are Red, Violets Are Blue,* and *1st to Die.* Only in *Four Blind Mice* does a genuinely happy relationship develop and then culminate in marriage. In the world of James Patterson, love is a risky thing—it more often leads to heartbreak than to living happily ever after.

HORROR

A frequent genre that Patterson utilizes in his Cross novels is horror, a type that begins with the gothic novel, described by British author and critic J. A. Cuddon as being "a tale intended to chill the spine and curdle the blood" (1991, 381). This genre relies to a great extent on setting, featuring such staples as hidden passages, tunnels, stairways that drop downward and meander into cobweb-festooned darkness, decaying mansions, hands that reach out to grasp one, and doors that slam suddenly behind one. *Along Came a Spider,* with its live burial of two small children on an abandoned farm, and *Kiss the Girls,* with its claustrophobic description of a many-layered series of underground cellars used to hold young women captive, are both superb examples of horror and the use of gothic settings, as is the description of the mental institution in *The Thomas Berryman Number,* of death row and a legal execution in *Four Blind Mice,* and of a prison for those sentenced to life terms in *2nd Chance.* Although I have noted throughout this Companion that as a general rule Patterson puts little emphasis on setting, when he turns his hand to the gothic he shows that he knows very well how to go about using setting to thoroughly frighten the reader.

SOCIOLOGICAL COMMENTARY

Another subgenre of popular fiction is the thesis novel, also known as the sociological novel. Works in this genre have as a significant aspect of the story the examination of issues current in the society at the time of their writing. For some authors the goal of such novels is to correct perceived injustices while for others the goal is simply to expose these injustices, to bring them to light. Superb examples of such sociological novels are Harriet Beecher Stowe's *Uncle Tom's Cabin* (1852) with its aching portrayal of slaves in pre-Civil War America, Charles Dickens' *Hard Times* (1854), a novel that highlights the conditions of the working class in the England of its time, and John Steinbeck's *The Grapes of Wrath* (1939), a work that today is still unsurpassed in the sharp realism of its portrayal of the bitter fate of Oklahomans who emigrated from the ravages of the dust bowl to the illusory promised land of California.

James Patterson's focus on social commentary arises from the fact that in the Alex Cross novels his protagonist is an African American police detective living in an inner-city neighborhood in Washington, D.C. All eight of Patterson's Cross novels have an element of such commentary, whether it is recognition of the fact that if one is African American it is almost inevitable that one is also color-conscious when interacting with the larger white society, that any romantic involvement with whites is taken as an open invitation for disparagement on the part of the society around one, and consistently in these novels, that in African American neighborhoods crime is accepted as the norm by a predominantly white power structure and, as such, is largely ignored. And while Patterson suggests no specific remedies for racism in America, his awareness of it and inclusion of it in his novels has the virtue of bringing it to the attention of a very wide readership, one that is reading for entertainment and would be unlikely to otherwise seek out literature critical of contemporary America.

3

The Thomas Berryman Number (1976)

The Thomas Berryman Number is James Patterson's first novel, and it is to date his greatest critical success, winning the Edgar Award for Best First Novel in 1977. This is a very highly regarded award named in honor of Edgar Allan Poe, considered by most critics to be the creator of the mystery and detective genre. It is given by the Mystery Writers of America in twelve categories of mystery and detective fiction, and what makes it particularly coveted is the fact that the award is given to a writer by his or her peers in the field. To be recognized by one's own is indeed an honor, equivalent for a mystery writer to an actor's winning an Oscar.

GENRE

Unlike Patterson's subsequent mystery novels, which fall largely into the police procedural category and, as such, feature professional detectives, *The Thomas Berryman Number* has an amateur detective, the investigative journalist Ochs Jones. This is a choice that works very well for Patterson since, as B. A. Pike notes, "Journalists rank high among those who legitimately go about asking questions and, so, are plausibly involved in criminal investigation" (1999, 244). It is a genre that has a long history, with one of the first journalist detectives appearing as early as

1908 (Gaston Leroux's Joseph Rouletabille). Although in its use of the amateur detective as protagonist it remains atypical of Patterson's work, *The Thomas Berryman Number* is my favorite of his novels. Ochs Jones is a man of empathy and intelligence, a reporter who brings the world of the crime and the people involved in it very much to life and, in doing so, keeps the reader enthralled. The novel also crosses over into the genre of true crime, since it is clearly (and specifically) related to the assassinations of Martin Luther King, Jr., John F. Kennedy, and Medgar Evers, with references to other real-life assassination attempts. There is a symbiotic relationship between true crime and fictional crime, most often seen as a spectrum moving from factual, police-blotter accounts to those which, while equally true, utilize fictional models. DeMarr says that Truman Capote's *In Cold Blood* (1965) is largely responsible for bringing respectability to the modern true crime genre. Capote's work "focuses on a gruesome murder; painstakingly re-creates the crime, its antecedents, and its aftermath; inquires into the minds and motives of the killers; and self-consciously employs novelistic techniques to convey lurid events" (2001, 857). Here, Capote is following the precedent set by Edgar Allan Poe in his short story "The Murder of Marie Roget" (*Snowden's Lady's Companion*, Nov. 1842), a fictional account based on "the mysterious death of an actual New York tobacconist, Mary Rogers" (Anderson-Boerger 1999, 469). Poe thus sets a precedent for the mystery and detective writers who will follow him. Where the genres of true crime and mystery and detective fiction differ is in structure, since in true crime novels the identity of the killer is usually known from the outset; DeMarr adds the distinction that "Most accounts contain an extensive report on the trial of the culprit, the point before which mystery novels usually conclude" (2001, 857). In contrast, in Patterson's novel, we think we know who the killer is, and yet we are kept on tenterhooks; the reversals Patterson has built into the plot in its identification of the guilty person leave the reader uncertain until the end. In addition, the almost-obligatory trial scene is missing from *The Thomas Berryman Number,* since although we finish the book knowing who the assassin is, there is no one left alive to bring to trial.

PLOT DEVELOPMENT

Plot development can usually be divided into four parts: the original situation, the complications, the crisis, and the denouement. The original situation is the world of the work of fiction before something happens to disrupt it. However, the plot for *The Thomas Berryman Number* is very complex, foreshadowing the complexity of the story that is to follow. Instead of beginning with what would normally be the original situation, the novel begins with a two-page prologue predating the events of the story by twelve years. The prologue introduces two characters, good friends Thomas Berryman and Ben Toy, who commit their first of many murders while hitchhiking to New York. In these few pages they are presented as witty, companionable, and utterly ruthless; and thus the prologue serves to alert the reader to the fact that no good will come of these two.

The original situation follows this prologue and adds to the complexity of the plot, since it is written in the form of a preface that is a flashback, in which Ochs Jones explains how he came to be involved in the investigation that makes up the story that will follow: "Four months ago, the thirty-seven-year-old mayor of our city, Jimmie Horn, was shot down under the saddest and most bizarre circumstances I can imagine" (6). Jones is the reporter who wrote the articles covering the assassination for Horn's hometown newspaper, the *Nashville Citizen Reporter,* articles that turn out to be wrong, although at this point the reader does not know why they're wrong—we are merely forewarned of this by Jones before we've even begun the novel proper. The presumed assassin is in turn killed by a professional hitman, introducing the reader to a world of Chinese boxes in which each seeming solution leads to another puzzle; in this case, the puzzle of why a hitman would be hired to kill an assassin who is in a crowd surrounded by police and who will obviously be arrested as soon as he commits his very public crime.

In terms of the second aspect of plot development, complications are something out of the ordinary, something that disrupt the day-to-day activities of the novel and create a situation that the characters must deal with in one way or another. Often, there is an initial major complication that puts into play a whole series of further complications. In *The Thomas Berryman Number,* such a major complication occurs when the *Citizen Reporter* receives a call from a New York psychiatrist who says "a patient of his had been talking about the Jimmie Horn shooting nearly a week before it happened" (7), and who has identified Thomas Berryman as the assassin. Because Jones had written articles on Horn in the past and because Horn was a personal friend, Jones is assigned by his editors to follow up on this development, although he sees it as a dead end (the assassination has been shown over and over again on television, and there seems to be no question about the fact that a man named Bert Poole is caught on camera shooting the gun that killed Horn). Jones feels that he is missing out on the main story of Horn's death, side-tracked to an implausible scenario constructed by an unreliable source. Thus, feeling sorry for himself, he begins his investigation at a mental hospital on Long Island, where the patient who is referred to in the phone call turns out to be Ben Toy, the friend of Thomas Berryman's introduced in the prologue. A fascinating series of interviews with Toy follows, in which he describes Thomas Berryman's life as a brilliant, highly regarded (within a specialized world) contract killer, and steers Jones to people who can confirm Toy's report on the real murderer of Jimmy Horn.

The climax of a story, novel, or play is its turning point and emotional high point; once the climax is introduced, nothing new will happen to alter the direction of the narrative. In the climax of Patterson's novel, Joe Cubbah, a killer-for-hire who has shot Horn's supposed assassin, supports Toy's scenario, saying that yes, Berryman committed the actual murder, using a silenced gun and shooting it through a jacket wrapped over his arm. Although Poole, the accused assassin filmed on video and shown nation-wide on television, did indeed shoot at Horn, his shots went wild. Berryman is in turn killed by Cubbah, who has been hired to remove any link between Berryman and the man who hired him to kill Horn.

Finally, the denouement presents the consequence or consequences of the action that has occurred in the climax and acts as a wrapping up of the story. *The Thomas Berryman Number* has a classic denouement in that all of the villains are accounted for and brought to justice of one kind or another: the would-be assassin is dead, his killer is in prison, Berryman is dead, his friend Ben Toy will probably spend the rest of his life (which may not be very long, since he is suicidal) in mental hospitals, and the person who hired Berryman to kill Jimmy Horn is also dead, albeit of natural causes. The reader knows who killed whom and why, and this complex story is brought to resolution.

CHARACTER DEVELOPMENT

As a general rule, Patterson's main characters tend to be complex or multi-dimensional, and at the same time, they remain static, or non-changing; this pattern is true of *The Thomas Berryman Number* as well as of the later novels covered in this book. The hero or protagonist is Ochs Jones, a reporter for the *Nashville Citizen-Reporter*, and we know a good deal about him. We know that he is a good writer, since his earlier essays on Jimmy Horn, the victim in this novel, have earned awards and are the reason that his editors assign him to this off-the-wall story with a severely disturbed mental patient as its source. His editors also respect his judgment; they support him on what might seem—and what he himself considers to be—a highly implausible investigation. Jones has a good marriage—he's been married to the same person since his second year in college—and he loves his two children, Janie Bug and Little Cat, who love him in return. He is also a compassionate person, a reporter who is well aware of how the press and the exposure it creates can intrude on people's lives. For this reason, in his articles he changes the names of witnesses who are marginally involved and are innocent of the killing. He does, however, lack self-knowledge. He says, "This book is mostly for my nine-year-old daughter Cat, I think" (4), and the reader is left wondering, "Why 'I think?' Is the book for Cat or isn't it? And why isn't it for Janie Bug, too?" He is also a static character. He says that he did not enjoy this investigation, although he thought that he would, but he does not explain why he didn't enjoy it, nor why he thought he would. In the absence of such an explanation, he ends the novel as he began it, an outstanding investigative reporter who tracks down every lead and conscientiously reports his findings, and on the evidence given here, should he be assigned another investigative story, he will proceed in exactly the same way.

The novel's villain or antagonist is Thomas Berryman, professional killer. Since Berryman is dead when the novel opens, it would seem that all the information on him would be hearsay. However, Patterson shifts from first person to third person (see the discussion on point of view, in the following section) and past to present throughout the novel, and this enables him to describe Berryman from many different perspectives, making him, like Jones, a multi-dimensional character. It is arguable that unlike Jones, Berryman is a dynamic character, one who changes from the beginning of the story to its end, although the evidence for this is slight. In terms of his personality, Jones says that the 29-year-old Berryman became a killer when he was 18, "a decision he made based on his executing several beautiful pronghorn antelopes and one Mexican priest" (4). The son of a circuit court judge, Berryman was very well liked in his hometown of Claude, Texas, where he was known as the Pleasure King, and Jones thinks of him that anyone who looked him in the face couldn't help but like him. Berryman justifies what he does by saying that being a professional killer gives him freedom, "too much freedom to stop now" and he explains that his philosophy is "fuck it all" (105). He is very good at his job, a meticulous planner who, until the Horn murder, has always succeeded. His killings are imaginative and vicious, those of a sociopath who simply does not see others as being as real as he is, and, consistent with the profile of the sociopath, he is cruel to animals; when pigeons land on the ledge of his New York apartment he amuses himself by burning their feathers and then, when they can no longer fly down to the ground, letting them starve. Berryman does, however, pride himself on the fact that he has never harmed a friend. His justification for accepting the contract to kill Jimmy Horn, a good man who has done him no injury, is that if he doesn't kill Horn, someone else will. Although he is supposed to be very intelligent (his I.Q. is 166), he does not anticipate that the man who has hired him to kill Horn has also hired another professional hitman to kill Berryman after the job is completed, and this atypical lack of anticipation is the flaw that brings about Berryman's death. It is also the evidence that suggests he is dynamic: he has gone from taking jobs that are 100 percent certain to taking one that, by his own evaluation, is only 99 percent certain, suggesting that this compulsive planner and researcher has become a risk-taker, although why this has happened is left unclear.

A third major character, also an antagonist, is Ben Toy, Berryman's best friend since their childhood in Texas. In this friendship, Toy sets the pattern for significant relationships that begin in childhood and that appear in subsequent Patterson novels, both among protagonists and antagonists, and always between two males. Toy has been an accomplice of Berryman's since Berryman's first killing, and we know a good deal about him; he was known in Claude as "the funniest man in America" (65), he is exceptionally handsome, and he is most likely incurably insane. As a boy he enjoyed wearing his mother's underwear, a detail suggesting that he showed evidence of being something other than normal even as a child. Over time he has become sickened by killing, although it is never clear why this change has occurred, why he has gone from Berryman's assistant to his opponent. It is Toy who attempts to report Berryman's coming assassination of Jimmy Horn, but the people he is reporting it to, his caretakers in a mental institution, do not take the threat seriously until after the event. Toy is the source for Jones's information on Berryman and, therefore, for the book itself, and he is a character who both fascinates readers and at the same time leaves them unsatisfied. He owns Toy's Flower and Toy Shop, which apparently sells flowers but no toys, and Jones says of him that whether or not he knew it, Toy hated Thomas Berryman, but Jones never explains why he thinks this, leaving the reader waiting and hoping for more. In terms of development, Toy is the novel's most dynamic character, moving from loyal accomplice and fellow killer to betrayer. As with Berryman, the specific motivating force or forces for this change are left open.

Another of the book's main players, in this case a second protagonist, is Jimmy Horn, the African American mayor of Nashville, Tennessee, who is Berryman's victim. Horn is running for senator and is considered certain to win, which is the ostensible motive for killing him. Like Berryman and Toy, Horn is well-developed, although he is a static figure—he doesn't live long enough to undergo character change. Throughout the novel he carries with him the aura of a figure in Greek tragedy, of someone doomed from the beginning. This is in part because readers know that he will indeed be killed. However, it is also a result of the many references made to Martin Luther King. Like King, Jr., Horn is a charismatic figure, a spellbinding speaker who is beloved by the African Americans in his state. Jones calls him "a driven man" who had "conditioned himself to be a successful black leader and spokesman" (141). There have been two previous attempts on his life and Horn says that he has become fatalistic about being killed and can even joke about it, although there is nothing funny about the killing when it does take place. Because of the clear association between Horn and King, when Horn is shot the message is that yet another fine human being, someone who could have done a great deal of good in the world, has been taken.

There is little information on Horn's wife and children, but each of his parents, his grocer father and school-teacher mother, is given a cameo appearance in which they are drawn as people of dignity and insight, wise in the ways of politics and human nature. Horn's mother becomes a model for Patterson's later creation, Nana Mama, who appears in all of the Alex Cross novels, and Cross himself shares many characteristics with Horn, including the fact that both are said to resemble the young Mohammed Ali.

There are a number of minor characters in the novel, all drawn with quick brushstrokes that give little detail as to the whole person but are successful in creating plausible outlines for the reader to fill in from past reading experience. Because of the lack of detail, these are stock characters, a term used to describe simplistic characters who have become conventions in different genres, such as the hard-boiled detective, the wicked witch, and the cruel stepmother. Six characters fall into this category. Bert Poole, the would-be assassin of Horn, is a disturbed, middle-class young man of limited intelligence who envisions becoming significant by killing a significant person. Oona Quinn, Berryman's girlfriend, is a beautiful young girl who apparently remains with him (she knows that he is a killer) because he represents a life of wealth and glamour that is far removed from her life as a salesgirl. Joseph Cubbah, a mob hitman hired to kill

Berryman, fits everyone's expectations of such a person by owning a candy store as a front and also by being a bookie. Jefferson Johnboy Terrell is the ex-governor of Tennessee and the epitome of a political wheeler-dealer who has hired both Berryman and Cubbah. Finally, Lewis Rosten and Moses Reed are Jones's superiors at his newspaper, men who are loyal and supportive and have integrity—indeed, they are everyone's boss of choice and bring to mind people such as Bill Bradley, the editor of the *Washington Post,* who supported his reporters Bob Woodward and Carl Bernstein through the months of their investigation into Nixon's Watergate scandal.

SETTING

In literature, setting means the scenery within which the characters in a work exist and the story takes place. Such scenery is both natural and artificial. Natural setting refers to those elements of setting that exist in the natural world (mountains, streams, forests, the weather, and so on). Artificial setting refers to those elements that are man-made (buildings and furniture, for example). Artificial settings also include the clothes an author dresses his or her characters in.

Setting can be used to show what a character is like (people often define themselves by how they dress and the kinds of houses they live in), to create a sense of atmosphere (a storm about to strike is a common way of suggesting that something terrible is about to happen), and even to show character motivation (there may be something in the setting, either natural or man-made, that causes a character to act in a particular way, such as extreme heat that frazzles everyone's tempers and drives some to actions they would not otherwise commit). A standard way of analyzing setting is to consider the impact of natural and man-made settings on a particular work. In *The Thomas Berryman Number,* for the most part setting plays a small role, serving to add plausible background detail rather than to impact plot events.

In terms of artificial setting, Berryman's Long Island beach house establishes his financial success as a professional killer, as does his New York apartment overlooking Central Park, properties far beyond the dreams of the average uneducated 29 year old. Since the interiors are only sketched in, neither place gives information on Berryman's character, his tastes, his sense of home. In the same way, Ben Toy's penthouse apartment is described only in terms of its cost, to again establish Berryman's success—it is Berryman who pays Toy. Joe Cubbah's candy store provides an expected setting for a mob member, and the country house that Jones rents to write his book on the assassination of Jimmy Horn is exactly the sort of retreat that readers associate with authors at work (for example, John Irvine's New Hampshire and Stephen King's Maine, where each author has chosen a non-urban, low-key American village to work in), and in this way setting adds credibility to Ochs's role as a writer—this is where writers go to do their work.

As a general rule, then, in *The Thomas Berryman Number* setting adds credibility rather than dimension to character or motivation to action. There are, however, three exceptions to this: the mental institution where Ben Toy is a patient, Ben Toy's flower shop, and Thomas Berryman's father's home. In the mental institution Toy is in a seclusion room, a room "used for patients who act-out violently . . . against the staff, or other patients, or themselves" (16). Toy, Jones is told, has acted out against all three. The room is claustrophobic, a very small room with bars and metal screens on its windows. Its only furniture is a mattress, and its bareness and size work to convince the reader that yes, there is something very, very wrong with Ben Toy. This is underscored by the description of Toy's shop, a florist shop that he owns as a hobby and as "something he felt made him more than just a wiseass cowboy with a few dollars to throw around" (28). The shop was his bid for normalcy but now it is filled with dead and rotting flowers that have been neglected for weeks, signaling all that has gone awry in Toy's life. He has abandoned the shop, just as he has abandoned Berryman—Toy has no more dreams or ambitions and, like the dead flowers, it is impossible to see him coming back to a sane life.

Berryman's father, Judge Berryman, lives in the midst of a scene that is equally foreboding, and here, both natural and artificial settings have turned against what is fruitful and life-giving. His house is sprawling and ramshackle, the garden and pool overgrown. "The whole area is ugly, almost supernaturally ugly and sad" (167). Everything here is rotting, diseased and dying, and nature has gone wild, taking over the man-made settings. Berryman's father is very near death, and is described as something inhuman: in his wheelchair he looks to Berryman like a boulder, "a rolling tombstone" (168). In one of the novel's most bizarre scenes, the father is so delighted to see his son that he grabs a garden toad and eats it. Berryman's roots lie here, at his father's home, and they are clearly rotten and twisted like the land they've grown out of.

POINT OF VIEW

Patterson's point of view in *The Thomas Berryman Number*—that is, the perspective from which the novel is told—shifts throughout from first person, through the eyes of Ochs Jones, who speaks in the "I" voice, to third person omniscient, in which an unknown narrator who can see into the minds of all the characters tells the story. Presenting Jones's sections of the novel in first person works well, since the reader comes to know Jones and to identify with his investigation, to share his confusion and to come to full understanding of the assassination at the same pace as Jones. In this way, the reader too is an investigative reporter, assembling bits of knowledge from many different people, following leads as they come up, slowly making sense of an implausible story that has three different killers focused on a single event. However, there is much that Jones cannot know, such as John Jefferson Terrell's political maneuvering, and having these details in the novel provides motive and credibility to the assassination. Since Terrell is unlikely to divulge this information, third person omniscient is a useful technique for credibly including it in the narrative. Between these two points of view, the reader gains Jones's knowledge as well as knowledge that is outside of his awareness, helping to fully develop the picture of what has happened to Jimmy Horn.

As well as shifting points of view, in *The Thomas Berryman Number* Patterson also uses a shifting time sequence, going back and forth over the dates from the time Berryman is hired until his death. The novel goes from New York City in June of 1974 to West Hampton in July, then back to Lake Stevens, Washington, in a previous, unspecified year, then to New York City again in July of 1974 but, a few pages later, to New York City in June of that year. There is a jump to Nashville in early September, then back to Nashville in June, then to Nashville in October, back to Nashville in June, and so on, with side trips to Claude, Texas, White Geese, Kentucky, and Philadelphia, among other places. These shifts are difficult to follow—the reader keeps asking, "Where am I? When is this happening?"—but they are successful in that they show how an investigation of this sort skips around, how one interview takes an investigator back to earlier information and then forward to additional interviews arising from the new information. In this way, Patterson effectively mimics an actual investigation which is always moving through space and time, based on what is discovered and when it is discovered. Each new bit of information can lead forward or backward, or both, and this staccato, out-of-sequence pattern mimics Ochs Jones's description of investigative reporting in which he says that it consists of "a puzzle where all the pieces have been lost . . . in different places. Around the house, the backyard, the car, anywhere the car may have been since the puzzle was bought" (38). The task of the investigative reporter is to go to each of these places to ferret out the pieces. This description is as true in real life as in fiction, but it is difficult to successfully control in fiction since readers of popular literature tend to have a low tolerance for confusion (if they cannot follow a story they are likely to abandon it), and it speaks to Patterson's skill as a writer that he can handle so many different time periods and locations and still pull events together into a coherent whole.

THEMATIC ISSUES

A major theme in *The Thomas Berryman Number* is that human beings are inevitably vulnerable, despite the efforts we make to be invulnerable. This theme appears in the character of Oona Quinn, who relies on her beauty as her identity and defense; but this beauty does not protect her, since she needs constant reassurance that she is indeed a very pretty woman, and she cannot cope without that reassurance. Jones says that he has changed her name in his report of this investigation to protect her from notoriety, but anyone who reads his report will be able to track her down through the other information included in it. (As just one example, the people who worked for Thomas Berryman surely know her correct name, and how long would it take someone to get to Ben Toy and learn her true identity?) Vulnerability is also apparent in the life of Jefferson Johnboy Terrell, who has hired both Berryman and Cuddah, first to protect himself against the political power of Jimmy Horn and then to guard against retaliation from Berryman. Horn and Berryman do end up dead, but so does Terrell, who dies of a presumed heart attack just as he is about to go to trial for his role in Horn's murder. Terrell has depended on his past as an ex-Governor of Tennessee to protect him but instead it targets him as a most likely suspect in the assassination plot. In Cuddah's case, he has taken on the job of killing Berryman, counting on his expertise as a professional hitman as his protection. His expertise is of little use, though, when he is filmed on TV at the assassination site dressed in a dead state trooper's uniform. Thomas Berryman, master professional killer, who is brilliant and charming, relies on his concentration, organization, and research to guarantee his success in his kills, but these skills let him down—they are not sufficient to prevent his death at the assassination site. And finally Jimmy Horn, who has a very experienced security organization and who is surrounded by people who not only want to protect him but who also love him, turns out to be vulnerable. Even though he has survived two previous assassination attempts, he does not survive this one. Thus beauty, political power, and professional experience take one only so far, and ultimately, to be human is to be vulnerable.

ALTERNATIVE READING: THE WRITER'S TECHNIQUES

In *The Thomas Berryman Number*, James Patterson has set himself a difficult task; he needs to keep the reader interested in the unfolding story even though the reader knows who has been killed and, early on in the story, who did the killing. Patterson uses two basic techniques to sustain interest. First of all, he relates the death of Jimmy Horn to many other famous assassinations, and in this way, he plays on the public's fascination with such killings. There are references to Martin Luther King, Jr., to John F. Kennedy, to Jack Ruby and Lee Harvey Oswald, to James Earl Ray, to Medgar Evers, and to George Wallace throughout the text, giving the reader a factual context for the fictional killing in this novel. Jones calls the assassination a moral drama, and he says that even "one of the top redneck gin mills in the state of Tennessee has a fresh print of Jimmie Horn over the liquor" because "people are partial to moral drama" (5). This is an astute observation, and it explains why assassinations are visited and revisited in books, films, plays, and on television. They are a form of contemporary Greek tragedy, in which someone is doomed from the opening pages, and the audience waits to see the doom unfold. These events also speak to our contradictory need as a society to know what has happened and why, paired with what seems to be our innate tendency to believe that it is never possible to know what has happened with absolute certainty. In real life, this contradictory pattern appears over and over again; an article in *The Seattle Times* for April 4, 2002, reads, "The F.B.I. in Florida is looking into claims by a minister that his father, not James Earl Ray, was the triggerman in the 1968 assassination of the Rev. Martin Luther King Jr. . . . 'We are taking this very seriously,' agent Ron Grenier said" (A5). This pattern of ultimate uncertainty is mirrored in *The Thomas Berryman Number* when Jimmie Horn visits James Earl Ray and concludes that Ray did not kill Martin Luther King, and although this story line is not developed, the visit reinforces the theme that full knowledge is beyond us.

The other technique that Patterson uses to keep the reader enthralled is that of foreshadowing. J.A. Cuddon defines foreshadowing as

> The technique of arranging events and information in a narrative in such a way that later events are prepared for or shadowed forth beforehand. A well-constructed novel, for instance, will suggest at the very beginning what the outcome may be; the end is contained in the beginning and this gives structural and thematic unity. (1991, 350)

Patterson first uses foreshadowing in the novel's prologue, where both Berryman and Toy are established as killers long before the killing of Jimmy Horn took place, and then again in the preface, where Jones announces that he will write about the deaths of Horn and various other characters involved in the assassination, although of course Horn has not yet died.

Foreshadowing continues throughout the novel, most notably in Jones's frequent comments to the effect that he will make a mistake in judgment (he has not yet made this mistake), that Oona Quinn will turn out to be wrong in her reading of Berryman (she herself does not yet know this), that Jones will learn many unpleasant facts (he has not yet discovered them), that something frightening is in store for him (it has not yet happened), and that Jones and his editor are quite wrong in their assumptions about how the murder was planned (they do not, at this point in the novel, know that they are wrong). Each of these examples has the effect of keeping the reader turning pages: What is Jones's mistake? Why is Oona wrong about Berryman? What are the unpleasant facts Jones says he will find out? What frightening thing is in store for him? Why are Jones and his editor wrong? What is the right answer? A more subtle form of foreshadowing is in the title itself; Thomas Berryman refers to his killings as "numbers," so that, for example, the assassination of Jimmy Horn would be "The Jimmy Horn Number." At the end of the novel, an astute reader can put together this pattern with the book's title and determine that *The Thomas Berryman Number* can only refer to the killing of Thomas Berryman, a foreshadowing of what will happen to him. The novel does come through with answers to all of the questions raised by the foreshadowing technique, and for this reason, readers have confidence that if they keep reading, everything will be revealed. Despite the fact that victim and killer are identified beforehand, there are still many small mysteries to be solved, along with the promise that they will be solved if only the reader continues on.

4

Along Came a Spider (1992)

Along Came a Spider represents a number of firsts for James Patterson; it is the first of his novels for which he designed the marketing plan, utilizing the skills he had gained as a professional working in the advertising field at its top levels, and it is also his first best seller, which speaks well for both his writing and his marketing talents. In addition, it is his first novel to introduce Alex Cross, a Washington, D.C., homicide detective who becomes an on-going character in a series that so far totals eight novels. *Spider* is, however, the second of Patterson's novels to use a line from a nursery rhyme for its title (the first is 1979's *See How They Run*), a pattern that he has followed since with 1995's *Kiss the Girls,* 1996's *Jack & Jill,* 1998's *When the Wind Blows,* 1999's *Pop! Goes the Weasel,* 2000's *Roses Are Red,* and 2001's *Violets Are Blue.*

This use of a pattern format for titles works well to establish author recognition for readers, so that they can say, "*Violets Are Blue*—oh, that must be by the person who wrote *Roses Are Red.*" Creating brand recognition is probably second nature for someone with Patterson's advertising background. However, it is also a device with a respected tradition in mystery and detective fiction. Agatha Christie, the superb Golden Age mystery writer (1890–1976), made use of such titles as *And Then There Were None* (1940), *Hickory, Dickory, Dock* (1955), and *A Pocket Full of Rye* (1954), and she is only one of many writers who have adopted this format. Lucy Rollin, writing in *The Oxford Companion to Crime and Mystery Writing,* says of nursery rhymes as titles, "The ironic contrast between their lilting rhymes and jolly rhythms and the mayhem they describe suggests not only a similar irony in a crime novel but the elemental pleasure to be had in reading it" (1999, 315). Thus, Patterson is well within an established popular literature tradition in his references to these rhymes.

Finally, another first for Patterson is that in *Along Came a Spider* he abandons the use of the amateur detective that worked so well for him in *The Thomas Berryman Number* and uses instead a professional detective in a police procedural format, with Alex Cross as the central figure. Patterson retains, though, the use of real-life crime as a catalyst to the fictional crime of the novel, in this case, the kidnapping and murder of Charles Lindbergh's baby. As in *Berryman,* such use of an actual crime lends plausibility to the novel's horrifying scenario of the kidnapping and live burial of two children.

GENRE

Along Came a Spider is primarily a police procedural, "the subgenre of mystery and detective fiction in which the mystery is solved by the police as part of their professional duties" rather than being solved by a brilliant private detective such as Sherlock Holmes (Kotker, 2001, 617). As is typical of this subgenre, there is much emphasis on the realistic life of the policeman—Cross's relationship with his partner, with his superiors, and with professionals in other agencies is a key motif just as it would be in the life of any working policeman. It is also typical of the procedural to show policemen in their private lives, emphasizing the danger, the low pay and the long hours, and the effect that this has on their families. In Cross's case, there are a number of scenes describing how often he must be away from his children and his feelings of guilt about this.

To a lesser extent, Patterson also makes use of the romance genre in his procedurals, although in *Spider* he inverts the formula. Rosenberg and Herald define this genre's basic theme as "true love triumphant against all odds" (1991, 143), but in the case of Cross's relationships, it turns out to be "true love defeated." Thus Cross, who has lost his wife in a drive-by shooting three years before the action of the novel, falls in love with a Secret Service agent working on the case with him. This relationship is a strong sub-plot in the novel, one that ends with Cross's betrayal by his supposed lover.

The gothic genre is also a strong element in *Spider,* helping, through its use of setting, to create an "atmosphere of brooding and unknown terror" (Holman and Harmon 1992, 219). Patterson creates precisely this atmosphere in his descriptions of the abandoned, derelict Maryland farm where the kidnapped children are imprisoned, and in particular, in the horrifying details he gives of their being buried alive. His antagonist's memories of being locked in a dark cellar for days on end when he was a child have the same chilling effect, and add to his monstrosity: how could someone tortured in this way turn around and do the same thing to another child?

Another genre element of *Spider* is its use of horror. This is an inclusive genre, dealing with "murder, suicide, torture, fear and madness" (Cuddon 1991, 417), all elements that apply to *Spider's* psychopathic antagonist, a man who has killed some 200 people not because of any harm they have done him (often they are strangers to him) but because of his compulsion to kill. Terrified over and over again as a child by a classic wicked stepmother, he has become a murderous and possibly suicidal adult.

Finally, Patterson makes use of the sociological genre in *Spider.* Novels in this genre concentrate "on the nature, function and effect of the society in which characters live" (Holman and Harmon 1992, 448), an element Patterson uses in his African American protagonist's awareness of and bitterness about the treatment of crime in the ghetto compared to its treatment in well-to-do D.C. neighborhoods; in the former, the African American Cross's supervisors see crime as a natural part of life, something that requires only cursory investigation, while in the latter it seen as an aberration that must be investigated, solved, and eliminated.

While this use of elements from many different genres would seem to make *Spider* a cross-genre novel, the fact that the central character is a policeman and that the crimes investigated follow general police routine places it most accurately in the police procedural category. Here, Patterson is following a model originally set by John Ball in his Virgil Tibbs novel *In the Heat of the Night* (1965). Like Ball, Patterson is a white author who has created an African American police detective who works—and must function in—a predominantly white bureaucracy.

PLOT DEVELOPMENT

Along Came a Spider opens with a prologue dated 1932, 60 years before the action of the novel. This is a pattern that Patterson also used in *Thomas Berryman,* and in both cases its purpose is to foreshadow that something is very wrong. Here, a 12-year-old boy is approaching the house of Charles Lindbergh, the aviation pioneer who was the first to perform a solo flight across the Atlantic, a feat that made him a popular hero throughout the world. Lindbergh's child, a beautiful, golden-haired baby boy, was kidnapped and then found dead in a crime that became known as "the crime of the century." The boy in the prologue goes through all the steps of kidnapping the Lindbergh baby and then burying him alive. The reader is left wondering if the boy actually was the Lindbergh kidnapper, or if this is a terribly disturbed fantasy of his.

The timeline then jumps to 1992 and establishes the original situation wherein two Washington, D.C., homicide detectives are investigating the slaying and mutilation of two African American prostitutes and a baby, a crime that in its brutality gives all the signs of being the work of a psychopath. Complications occur when two children of very well-to-do and politically powerful white families are kidnapped from their private school and the homicide detectives are taken off the prostitute case and assigned to the kidnapping. The detectives, African American partners John Sampson and Alex Cross, resent this change in assignment since in their view it underlies a police attitude that rates crimes against whites as being more significant than crimes against African Americans. Nonetheless, as professionals they are determined to give the kidnapping their best efforts.

Usually, the climax of a mystery story is the moment when the reader learns who the criminal is. In *Along Came a Spider,* however, the criminal is known from the outset: he is Gary Soneji, one of the teachers at the children's school, and his motive appears to be straightforward—he seeks a ransom of $10 million. He drugs the children and buries them in a pit in the ground that he has equipped with an oxygen supply. As he does this he is, at least in his estimation, copying the Lindbergh baby kidnapping, a crime that has fascinated him since he was a boy. Matters become more complex when one of the kidnapped children, the boy, is discovered dead, floating in a river. He has been physically and sexually abused. The girl is still missing and the ransom demand stays at $10 million. The kidnapper insists that Cross deliver the ransom, although Cross has no idea why he has been chosen, since he has never met Soneji. The ransom is delivered as instructed but the little girl is not returned and her whereabouts remains unknown. Soneji is arrested and claims that he is the victim of multiple personality disorder, that the real kidnapper is an alternate personality and that he has no knowledge of what this personality has done with the girl. As all of this is happening, a subplot describes the developing relationship between Cross and Jezzie Flanagan, a Secret Service agent who is the supervisor of the men who were supposed to be guarding the children.

Meanwhile, a witness connects Soneji to the murder of the prostitutes, and Cross, who is a psychologist, is put back on the case to create a psychological profile of Soneji. He hypnotizes him and decides that Soneji may indeed be suffering from multiple personality disorder. Cross's conversations with Soneji are one of the most interesting parts of the novel, reflecting Patterson's thorough knowledge of the field of psychiatry (as a student, he spent summers working at one of the finest mental institutions in the country).

With regard to the kidnapping, Soneji claims to have received none of the ransom money, and says that when he returned to the burial scene to retrieve the little girl, she was gone. Patterson has now created two new mysteries: who took the child and where is the money? As it turns out, the two Secret Service Agents responsible for the children realized that they were being followed by Soneji, a would-be kidnapper. They allowed him to go through with his plan and then intercepted the ransom drop-off. One of the agents is killed by Soneji, who has by now escaped from prison, and one is arrested.

In the climax, Jezzie Flanagan is revealed as the mastermind behind the ransom interception. She has had an affair with Cross only as a means of being able to know exactly what was transpiring in the investigation. She reveals the whereabouts of the little girl and, as in the classic mystery, all is now known: the identity of the kidnapper and the criminals who followed him, and the whereabouts of the child. In the denouement Soneji is re-captured, all the criminals are punished (Flanagan receives the death penalty, and in a macabre scene, she dies by lethal injection in Cross's presence), and the novel ends on a note of ominous foreshadowing when it is revealed that Soneji has already suborned a guard in the prison. Since this is how he went about escaping when he was first captured, the suggestion is that he will be on the loose again, perhaps to reappear in a subsequent James Patterson novel.

CHARACTER DEVELOPMENT

Alexander Isaiah Cross is the main character and the protagonist or hero of this novel. He is both well-rounded and dynamic, since we know a good deal about him—more than any other character in the book—and there is evidence that he changes in the course of the novel. Cross was orphaned when he was nine years old and then was taken in by his grandmother, whom he always refers to as Nana Mama, since she was (and is) both mother and grandmother to him. He has two brothers who were placed with other relatives, and he seems to have no contact with them, nor does he appear to want to have such contact, although no reason is given for this. Cross is 38 years old, six foot three, and a handsome man: he looks like the young Mohammad Ali (as does Jimmy Horn in *Thomas Berryman*—an interesting carry-over on Patterson's part from one novel to another). His dream was to be a practicing psychologist, something he should surely have been able to achieve with his doctorate from prestigious Johns Hopkins University. However, once he went into practice he found that whites distrusted a black psychologist and blacks couldn't afford one, and so he went into the police, an area where he could put to good use his knowledge of human nature. Cross is now a homicide detective in the Washington, D.C., police force, with the rank of Divisional Chief. He had a good marriage to Maria, a social worker, and he has been depressed ever since she was killed in an unsolved drive-by shooting. Cross is a very good father to Damon and Janelle, his six-year-old son and four-year-old daughter, and it is clear that they love him dearly. He is also a socially conscious member of his community; he lives in Washington's Southeast, a high-crime, ghetto neighborhood, and donates time two or three days a week to the food kitchen run by St. Anthony's Church, where he also does counseling in a prefab trailer with a sign that says, "The Lord helps them what helps themselves. Come on the hell in" (158). He loves jazz, and plays a "slightly out-of-tune, formerly *grand* piano" (9; italics in original) to relax.

Patterson has said of his use of an African American protagonist, "I was interested in creating a larger-than-life African American hero, because I didn't think there were many. Cross is raising two kids by himself, he has a great relationship with his grandmother; he's a trained psychologist who is also a detective; he's fearless and a little too obsessive about his work. He has his downsides, but he's bigger than life" (Frumkes 2000, 13).

Cross is also, in *Along Came a Spider,* drawn as a dynamic character. Initially a man who prides himself on his knowledge of others, he must come to terms with the fact that he was thoroughly deceived by Jezzie Flanagan, to the point of falling in love with her. He says to his partner Sampson, "You meet somebody who can lie to you the way she did, it changes your perspective on things. This is very tough to handle, man." Then, showing just how uncertain he now is of his own judgment, he says to Sampson, his best friend since childhood, "You ever lie to me?" (423).

Such a question would be unthinkable for the Cross who first appears in the novel, and it is indicative of just how damaging his relationship with Flanagan has been for him that he can ask it of Sampson.

John Sampson, Alex Cross's partner, is the other major protagonist of the novel, a positive character who can always be relied on by Cross. While it is clear that there is real affection and respect between the two partners, Sampson is nonetheless a flat character, in that the reader knows little about him, and a static character, in that he remains the same throughout the novel. His official rank is Senior Detective and he is obviously an imposing figure, standing six foot nine. (Next to him, the six-foot-three Cross feels small.) Sampson is a good friend to Cross, always willing to listen, he has a good sense of humor, he wears Wayfarer sunglasses, and this is about all that the reader knows of him. His education, his motivation for becoming a policeman, and his private life are all missing, leaving a stock character who is the partner everyone would wish to have, and who remains the same at the end of the novel as he was at the beginning.

Regina Hope, Cross's grandmother, is the final strong, positive character introduced in *Along Came a Spider.* A well-rounded character, she is testy and sharp-tongued, and, at age 79, still does volunteer work at a school in the Southeast even though she is retired from her job as assistant principal of a junior high school. She is a fleshed-out version of the mother of Jimmy Horn, a character Patterson introduced in *The Thomas Berryman Number,* who is also a school teacher, and also a source of wisdom. Hope, always known to Cross and his children as Nana Mama, has, with the death of Cross's wife, taken on the role of mother figure for the Cross children. It is she who maintains the household and is the source of stability for the children, given the exigencies of a policeman's profession. Her philosophy is that African Americans persevere, too often in silence, and that most whites are not to be trusted: "I would like to [trust them] but I can't. Most of them have no respect for us. . . . That's their way, at least with people they don't believe are their equals." She adds, "I'm not proud of these feelings I have, but I can't help them, either" (309). Her honesty makes her the novel's center of integrity; hers is the voice of wisdom and experience, one that remains constant throughout the story.

Along Came a Spider's primary antagonist or villain is the psychopath Gary Soneji, also known as Gary Murphy. Besides Cross he is the novel's only other well-rounded character, although unlike Cross, Soneji is static, remaining the same from the beginning to the end of the novel. There is a good deal of information on Soneji's childhood, all lending credibility to Patterson's description of him as a psychopath. His mother died when he was young and he was tormented by his stepmother, who shut him in a dark basement when he misbehaved (or whenever the whim struck her). Later in life, Soneji revenges himself by killing his stepmother, his step-siblings, and his father in a house fire, repeating here the classic psycho-pathic pattern of an abused child who in turn becomes an abuser of others. Since then, he says, he has killed more than 200 people, although the details on these deaths are absent from *Spider.* Soneji is a true crime fan who is particularly fond of kidnapping cases—as a child, he had an on-going fantasy in which he committed the Lindbergh kidnapping, a crime that actually happened 25 years before he was born. He says that it is this fantasy that kept him from going insane, a comment that highlights Soneji's limited self-knowledge since, on the evidence in the novel, there is no question of his going insane—he is already more than there.

As an adult, Gary Soneji's ambition is to be "America's first serial kid-napper" (31) and to this end he has, he says, been planning to kidnap somebody famous "since—well, since forever" (56). He is very intelligent and is capable of great charm: his wife, his child, and the children at the school where he teaches all love him. Soneji is also a most convincing character; when he is arrested for the kidnapping of the children, he claims as his defense that he suffers from multiple personality disorder, and it is virtually impossible to determine whether or not this is true, although Cross believes that Soneji is and has always been only one personality, that of Soneji, and his claims to the contrary are simply a brilliant, con-vincing defense. Soneji ends the novel as he began it, a victim stalking victims and, back in prison, an inmate who continues in his attempts to manipulate the prison system.

The remaining antagonists all enter the novel in the guise of protago-nists, since they are Secret Service agents and the reader has as yet no knowledge that they have gone bad. These are Mike Devine and Charlie Chakely, the agents charged with protecting the kidnapped children, and their supervisor, Jezzie Flanagan. The information on Devine and Chakely is minimal—there is no rationale given for why they have turned into criminals rather than crime fighters, although the reader is told that De-vine and Flanagan have had a long-standing affair. Flanagan plays the largest role of the three and is the most developed. She is a very attractive blonde who is good at her job, and she is proud of the fact that she is the first woman to hold a supervisor position in the Secret Service. She has worked hard to get to this position, earning a law degree with honors from the University of Virginia, a school that is one of the finest in the country. The child of alcoholics, Flanagan is a survivor and it is never clear to the reader what her motivation is in turning criminal—since her joy is derived from her job, it is hard to understand why she risks it all in a manner that can be traced back to her, something she herself, as an investigator, has to recognize could happen. The only hint that there is more to Flanagan than is apparent is her love of risk-taking, of riding her motorcycle at speeds over 100 miles an hour. She, like Soneji, is charming and convincing, and her love affair with Cross seems to be exactly that; the reader is as surprised as Cross to find that it was simply a ploy to allow Flanagan closer access to the investigation. She is a static or unchanging character and when she is executed for her responsibility in the death of the kidnapped child at the end of the novel, the reader accepts Cross's statement that like Soneji, she is a psychopath—it is as good an answer as any for what she has done.

SETTING

Along Came a Spider has three main settings: the Maryland farmhouse where the kidnapped children are buried, Cross's neighborhood in D.C., and a tropical island that Cross and Flanagan escape to from time to time, to leave the intensity of the investigation behind them. Of these, the most important is the artificial setting of the farmhouse. (See Chapter 3 for a discussion of artificial and natural settings.) With its run-down buildings and prepared burial site, it is, as noted before, a classic gothic site, one that terrifies the reader with images of being buried alive and not discovered until it is too late. In addition to underlining the horror of the children's situation, this setting also helps to define Soneji's character as one of utter ruthlessness and bizarre logic. There are many other places that kidnapped children could be hidden and to choose this particular one, with the elaborate life-support preparations it entails, is to truly define oneself as mad.

A second artificial or man-made setting, Cross's house on 5th Street in Southeast, is also a good example of the use of setting to establish genre conventions. The fact that the house is a small, older home underlines the procedural qualities of the novel, since this genre typically shows the police as overworked and underpaid, people unlikely to own posh homes in the suburbs. The home also adds to the development of Cross's character; it is cluttered and lived in, and by staying here Cross, who speculates that he really could leave the neighborhood and move to something more upscale and less crime-ridden, emphasizes his commitment to the neighborhood where he grew up. This reinforces his anger with his superiors when they take him off his original prostitution-murder case and assign him to the kidnapping—because he is committed to the neighborhood, he is also committed to taking the crime that routinely happens there as seriously as he takes crime happening anywhere in the city.

Finally, the natural setting of the tropical island acts as an ironic comment on the Cross-Flanagan relationship; this is paradise, only it is in paradise that Flanagan first betrays Cross by pretending to love him, and where he later traps her by secretly taping her confession to the kidnapping in the midst of an idyllic picnic for two on the beach. In the world of *Along Came a Spider,* paradise is only an illusion.

POINT OF VIEW

Patterson often uses multiple points of view in his novels, and he follows this pattern in *Spider,* shifting from first person, in which the reader is in the mind of Alex Cross and the story is told using the "I" voice, to third person, in which an unidentified omniscient narrator who can see into the minds of all the characters tells the tale. The "I" voice is a very effective technical device for this novel, in that it causes the reader to identify with Alex Cross throughout the investigation. When he is puzzled, the reader is puzzled; when he is angry, the reader understands the source of the anger; and when he is betrayed, the reader too feels betrayed, having experienced events as Cross has experienced them. Another advantage to the use of first person in *Spider* is that the reader, in identifying with the "I" voice, becomes an investigator along with Cross, and one of the delights of mystery and detective fiction for many readers is working out the solution to the crime in the same manner as the detective does. When Cross gathers evidence and that evidence is shared with the reader, the reader too can become a detective, seeking to find the solution by the same means as Cross.

In terms of the novel's use of third person, Holman and Harmon note that point of view "has often been considered the technical aspect of fiction that leads the critic most readily into the problems and meanings of a work" (1992, 367), and in *Spider,* the third-person sections work in exactly this way, although they are designed to mislead readers rather than to inform. Patterson puts his readers in the mind of a character and they naturally assume that they understand what that character is feeling and why. However, Patterson is most artful in his manipulation of this point of view so that, often, he presents just enough information to create the impression of opening a character's mind and exposing motivations when, in reality, he has left out significant details and so is actually leading readers astray while seeming to enlighten them.

An excellent example of such complex use of point of view is the character Jezzie Flanagan, who is thinking that she will bar from her mind images of the dead Goldberg child, that she will reject her feelings of guilt over his being kidnapped while she was responsible for his security. The reader automatically assumes that he or she now knows how Flanagan is reacting to the kidnapping, when in fact her guilt is based not on the fact that she was responsible for the child's safety and, by extension, his subsequent death, but instead, on her need to maintain her role of innocence. Her emotional reaction is for herself (guilt that she has made herself vulnerable) rather than for what has happened to the child. The scene can, of course, be read this way when it is initially presented. However, readers lack the background to understand the source of her guilt in the original scene; to understand it they would have to go back and re-read the novel, looking for previously unrecognized clues to Jezzie's responses. (Incidentally, many readers of mystery and detective fiction make a practice of doing exactly this, finishing a novel and then re-reading it to see how the author has set up and at the same time hidden the solution to a crime.)

Such use of third person omniscient, rather than creating overall knowledge of the plot for readers, actually misleads them: readers believe that they know what characters are doing and thinking when in actuality they lack the necessary information to know this. They only have the illusion of being in characters' minds. This is an excellent example of the use of point of view to obfuscate rather than to expose, and as such, it serves well in a mystery plot where the intent of the work is to puzzle readers and lead them astray.

THEMATIC ISSUES

Safety as an illusion is a central theme in *Along Came a Spider.* This is illustrated in a number of different ways in the novel. First of all is the death of Alex Cross's wife in a drive-by shooting. To date, the crime remains unsolved, suggesting that if the wife of a policeman can be murdered and no suspect apprehended, then no one is safe. The kidnapping of the two children also reinforces this theme, since they are the children of prominent families, attending an elite private school and protected to and from the school by the Secret Service. Nonetheless, the kidnapper succeeds in abducting them, showing that just as in the case of Cross's wife, official protectors are no guarantee of safety. Again, the children are taken by one of their teachers. One would assume that the sort of school they attend, where all the children are from privileged families, would be especially careful in screening its employees, but in fact, Gary Soneji has slipped through the mesh with false paperwork that could easily have been exposed with just a few phone calls.

If occupation and privilege fail as protectors, so too does intelligence. Soneji is said to be a brilliant man and a skilled planner, and yet all of his careful work, his testing of medications, of grave sites and of air supplies, fails in the face of the kidnapped Michael Goldberg's health history, so that Soneji ends up not with the ransom victim he had hoped for, but with a corpse.

Knowledge of human beings and their behavior patterns also provides no hedge against vulnerability. Cross, a psychologist, is never absolutely certain whether or not Soneji suffers from multiple personality disorder and therefore whether he should be treated for his illness or executed for his activities. More to the point, Cross is unable to detect that Flanagan is manipulating him. Surely a trained psychologist should be able to determine this, and the fact that Cross, drawn as a very intelligent man with an extensive background and superb education, cannot do so suggests that there is little protection to be gained from such specialized knowledge. Ultimately, the message here is that society is at the mercy of sociopaths such as Soneji and Flanagan.

Finally, the fact that at the end of the story Patterson has left the fate of Soneji open and has prepared the groundwork for creating a sequel to *Spider* in which Soneji will again be out in the world, stalking his victims, leaves the reader without closure. Some crime is punished, some continues to exist, and ultimately, everyone is vulnerable regardless of power, position, or education. This is a grim view of reality, and it also one that is supported on all sides by the events reported in our daily papers. If the theme of the classic mysteries was that evil can, with intelligence and determination, be removed from the world, the theme of this mystery is that it will always be a part of the human scene and that while it may be eradicated in one guise, it will persist in others.

ALTERNATIVE READING: THE SOCIOLOGICAL NOVEL

A sociological novel is one that "concentrates on the nature, function and effect of the society in which characters live" (Holman and Harmon 1992, 448). It considers issues current in the society at the time of its writing, either in hopes of correcting them or simply with the goal of exposing them. Some classic sociological novels are Harriet Beecher Stowe's *Uncle Tom's Cabin* (1852), with its deeply moving portrait of slaves in pre-Civil War America; Charles Dickens's *Hard Times* (1854), with its vivid descriptions of the plight of the working class in Victorian England; and John Steinbeck's *The Grapes of Wrath* (1939), with its wrenching portrayal of Oklahomans who immigrated to California because of the ravages of the Dust Bowl.

As a sociological novel, *Along Came a Spider* exposes what it is like to be an African American in a predominantly white American society, focusing on such issues as the fact that if one is African American, one is always color-conscious when interacting with the larger white society, that if one is African American, any romantic involvement with a white is taken as an open invitation for comment and derision on the part of the greater society, and that in African American neighborhoods crime is both endemic and, to a large extent, ignored by a predominantly white power structure.

In terms of African Americans being color-conscious, Patterson treads lightly here, making his only overt comment when Alex Cross decides to wear an old Harris tweed jacket because "It was a murder day, and that meant I'd be seeing white people" (11). If he must be different and "other," he can at least dress in a way that is comforting and habitual to white society. (It is interesting to contrast Cross's focus on outer presentation with Walter Mosley's Easy Rawlins, another African American detective who is introduced in 1990's *Devil in a Blue Dress*. The first thing Rawlins notices about anyone of any race or nationality, in any context, is his or her skin color—clothes are secondary and are used to enhance skin color or provide a contrast with it.)

As to total strangers feeling free to comment on African American-white American romantic relationships, the ugliest example of this happens when Cross and Flanagan, holding hands, are crossing a parking lot on their way to a basketball game and from nowhere a voice shouts, "Nigger lover!" More of the same follows and despite Flanagan's telling Cross to ignore the three white men who are harassing them, he takes them on and knocks two of them down. The third backs off and apologizes, saying of his friend who acted as spokesperson, "He had too much to drink, mister. We all did. . . . Hell, we work with black guys. We got black friends. What can I say? We're sorry" (291). Of course this adds to Cross's stature in the reader's mind, since he can triumph in a three-on-one situation, but it also points up the race consciousness of the society and it is ironic that such racist comments come from people who know and work with African Americans. The underlying message is glum indeed—if we cannot learn to accept one another by shared life situations, what hope is there for our developing a truly equitable society in which we are all fellow citizens? Racism is again the focus of a scene at Flanagan's lake cabin, where a fiery cross is burned on her lawn. Nana Mama, the novel's voice of wisdom, tells Cross that she does not trust white people, and with scenes like these, this is surely an intelligent response to being African American in contemporary America.

The most telling aspect of *Along Came a Spider* as a sociological novel is its treatment of crime as it is handled in African American neighborhoods. At the beginning of the book, a crime is reported to the police by a woman who "had been up with the night-jitters. It comes with the neighborhood" (15). Two pages later, Cross visits the murder scene of two prostitutes in D.C.'s Southeast and says, "It was a bad part of what somebody had let become a bad city" (17). Readers are then told that in the past year, there were over 500 killings in the greater D.C. area and that of these, only 18 of the victims were white. This is obviously a deadly place to be African American, and the lack of concern on the part of the power structure is evident when Cross and Sampson are pulled off the killing of three African Americans so that they can supplement the team investigating the kidnapping of two well-to-do white children. As Cross notes, "Homicides in Southeast don't count for much in the greater scheme" (33). Later, when he and Sampson are assigned back to the Southeast murders, little progress has been made and no one cares. Cross says of the little boy who has been killed, "Mustaf had already been forgotten. I knew that would never happen with the two private-school children" (47), and when he says this, any literate reader knows that he is more than likely right.

As with most of the rest of us, Patterson has no suggestions for changing the system. Instead, his focus is on exposing its flaws, and in the case of *Along Came a Spider,* of showing how hard it is to grow up in America when one is poor and is seen as "other." To the extent that knowledge precedes remedy, his book is a good start on the problems of racism. Perhaps his readers will, through his characters, be more able to see one another as people rather than as types, bringing them closer in their perceptions to Cross, who sees all people as sharing a common humanity, and distancing them from Soneji, who sees himself as the only human in his universe.

5

Kiss the Girls (1995)

This is James Patterson's second Alex Cross book, and in terms of its structure, it is his best book in the Cross series. Patterson has linked all the disparate parts of *Kiss the Girls* so that they flow into one another and make smooth connections. He takes the death of a child at the beginning of the novel and relates it to Cross's determination to capture a serial killer at the end of the novel, rather than just leaving it there as a frightening opening. He also uses humor in ways that feel natural, that make the humor an extension of the events it is born of. See, for example, the country western song that Cross hears at the Washington Duke Inn in North Carolina: "One Day When You Swing That Skillet, My Face Ain't Gonna Be There" (84). If this isn't a real song, then it certainly ought to be, and this is surely the setting in which one could expect to hear it. Observations of characters are equally sharp and precisely drawn so as to visually include the reader; when Cross and his partner Sampson visit a crime scene, he says, "At least half of the group were dressed in dark business suits. It was as if we had come upon some impromptu camping trip for an accounting firm" (61).

As is usual with his Cross novels, there is a strong love story as part of the plot, and in *Girls* it is absolutely credible; when the couple end the relationship, it is for reasons that are intelligent and loving, that leave them as dear friends, rather than because of an abrupt traumatic event brought in as a *deus ex machina,* or device from the blue, to resolve a situation that an author has finished with and wants to leave behind. And in terms of character, it is Patterson's most sensitive portrait of Cross as an African American in white America, showing his awareness of his color and, in his acceptance of it, his ability to overcome through intelligence, talent, and force of character the problems it creates for him. These aspects add up to a work that is Patterson's best example of the writer as a wordsmith—a skilled user and manipulator of the written word.

GENRE

As is true of all the novels in the Alex Cross series, *Kiss the Girls* is a police procedural in which crimes are solved by the police going about their usual routines rather than being solved by brilliant amateurs in the Nero Wolfe and Sherlock Holmes mold (see Chapter 2 for a more complete discussion of this and the following genres). There is much detail on the day-to-day life of police involved in a particular investigation, and especially on the conditions of the job and the negative effect that this has on family life. This effect is somewhat mitigated in *Girls,* though, since Alex Cross's initial involvement in the case comes about through the abduction of his beloved niece, and everyone in the extended family is grateful to have the skilled Cross involved in her search. Patterson also explores the rivalries between various law enforcement agencies, especially the hostility of most police forces toward the FBI and the arrogance of the FBI toward those same forces. He comes down heavily on the side of the local police through the device of having individual FBI agents drawn as good guys who make negative comments about their fellow agents, a technique that gives added credibility to the local police observations; if even some F.B.I. members themselves are skeptical of the agency, then surely the police are wise to share in this. So, when Cross tells his friend, agent Kyle Craig, "I don't agree with your people in Washington," Craig responds with, "Who does agree with Washington?" Cross also notes here that a nickname for FBI Quantico headquarters among its own agents is Disneyland East (365). This description of inter-agency rivalry and lack of cooperation is a convention of the police procedural, and is used to underline the difficulty of the work of average police officers—they have to fight their own and federal bureaucracies as well as the criminal on the street.

Another convention of the police procedural that Patterson includes here is the concept that evil is never eradicated, that when one case is over, there will be many others still awaiting resolution and that this is what being in the police is all about. Thus, in *Kiss the Girls*, the final lines of the novel are John Sampson, Cross's long-time partner, knocking on his door at three thirty in the morning with the message, "There's been a murder. . . . This one is a honey, Alex" (458).

One not-so-usual aspect of *Kiss the Girls* is Patterson's inclusion of conventions of the traditional, golden-age mystery developed by such masters of the genre as Agatha Christie (1890–1976), which he does when he has Cross enumerate what needs to be done: "There were three clues that I considered essential to solving the case. I reviewed them . . . as I drove" (301). The reader can almost hear Christie's famous detective Hercule Poirot saying these words. Cross also makes a point of creating lists of the known and unknown, of answers and questions to be answered, and these too echo the investigative devices of the classic detectives, whose reliance on diagrams, lists, and timetables were the tools that led them to solutions.

Because Alex Cross, Patterson's protagonist, is an African American, the Cross novels also fit into the genre of the sociological novel, in which a story looks at the effect of the overall society on the individual characters. This aspect is particularly well developed in *Kiss the Girls;* the location of the kidnapping is North Carolina, where Cross is not only an outsider but also an African American in the American South. He comments that this is his first time in the South since he was nine years old, and his apprehension about how he will be treated says much about race relations in modern America.

As he has in the first Cross novel, Patterson again incorporates devices of the gothic novel, with its emphasis on settings that create fear and an ominous sense of foreboding. Finally, this is also a work of suspense that makes fine use of the race-against-the-clock device that is classic in this genre (will the killers be discovered in time to save the remaining victims?), and it is also an example of the psychopathic killer subgenre that begins with John Fowles's *The Collector* (1963) and has been brilliantly developed by Thomas Harris in *The Silence of the Lambs* (1988). In this subgenre, a man who appears outwardly normal has a crazed inner fantasy world centered on the capture of young women. He never perceives these women as real, as having separate lives outside his fantasies of them. The terror of such novels lies in the women's desperate attempts to force their captors to see them as people like them, as people who exist apart from the fictional world the psychopath has created for them. An underlying assumption of such works is that if the psychopath could see his victim as being like himself he could let the victim go. A second underlying assumption is that such recognition is not possible for the psychopath—if it were, he would not have taken the victim captive in the first place—and therefore, in the absence of outside help, the victim is doomed. Whether or not that outside help will appear is the determining factor in what will be the ultimate outcome. Sometimes, as in *The Collector,* there will be no outside help; sometimes, as in *The Silence of the Lambs,* that help arrives. The fact that both of these outcomes are equally likely adds to the tension of this type of suspense novel.

PLOT DEVELOPMENT

James Patterson has a fondness for beginning his works with prologues that he uses to set a tone of fear and also of character and motivation on the part of his killers, and true to form, *Kiss the Girls* begins in this way. Its prologue is entitled "Perfect Crimes" and consists of two parts: "Casanova," the character who will turn out to be one of the novel's two serial killers, and "The Gentleman Caller," who will be the second of the killers. The story then skips ahead 13 years to the first chapter, set in Alex Cross's home in the impoverished, predominantly African American Southeast section of Washington, D.C. This shift in time is mirrored by shifts in setting and also in solutions; Patterson is a master of the answer that turns out to be a non-answer, as he demonstrates over and over in his Cross novels.

In *Kiss the Girls,* the main story opens with Cross rushing an 11-year-old boy who has attempted suicide to the hospital. The child is a drug runner, a seller of crack and a caretaker of dope addicts, living in a crack house with his addicted parents whose only interest in him is in exploiting him. He has come to the psychologist Cross for help and now, in despair, has cut his wrists and his throat. A neighbor alerts Cross but it is too late; the child dies in the hospital. This original situation is a very effective opening since it establishes that Cross is known and trusted in the neighborhood, that he is seen as a savior, and that even he can fail. It creates a sense of trepidation for the reader, since the rest of the novel will concern victims who have been captured to fulfill the needs of their captors and if Cross could fail once, perhaps he will fail in saving these victims, too.

Complications occur when Cross returns home to find that his 22-year-old niece Naomi, a law student in North Carolina, has been missing for four days. The story line then shifts away from D.C. and to the point of view of the serial killer who has kidnapped Naomi and is now stalking another woman. Cross goes to North Carolina and finds that Naomi is only 1 of 8 to 10 women who are missing: "All young. . . . All students in college or high school. Only two bodies have been found, though" (57), which raises the question of whether or not the remaining victims are still alive, and if so, for how long. Because they cross state lines the crimes are under FBI jurisdiction, and Cross is invited to take part in the investigation since he is well-known as an investigator and profiler of serial killers based on his earlier work with the psychopath Gary Soneji. Cross is so well-known that he has been invited to join the FBI's Behavioral Sciences unit, the group responsible for investigating such crimes. This FBI connection is vital to Cross's work in the South—without it, as an African American and a policeman from another jurisdiction, he would be given no access to any of the evidence despite his expertise and his relationship to one of the victims.

The events of the novel now shift from the East Coast to the West Coast, with intermittent stops in D.C. On the East Coast, the spree killer Casanova continues to stalk victims to add to his harem; on the West Coast a second spree killer, The Gentleman Caller, stalks victims, kills them, and takes various body parts as souvenirs. Cross discovers, through contact with a Los Angeles reporter, that Casanova and The Gentleman Caller are in communication with one another and postulates that they are an example of a psychological phenomenon known as twinning, a relationship "caused by an urge to bond, usually between two lonely people. Once they 'twin,' the two become a 'whole'; they become dependent on each other, often obsessively so. . . . In its negative form, it was the fusing of two people for their own individual needs, which weren't mutually healthy" (243). Later in the novel Cross notes of such pairs that once they have established such a relationship, they can no longer survive without each other. This is a fascinating detail, especially when looked at in light of Cross's statement that he and Sampson also are twinning, suggesting not only that Cross is deeply dependent on his partner but also that such twinning can have a positive aspect.

Ultimately, the two killers join one another in Casanova's East Coast harem, Cross and Sampson discover the lair, and The Gentleman Caller is killed in a shoot-out with them. Casanova escapes, still unidentified. The crisis then seems to have been reached when a Professor Wick Sachs is arrested and charged with being Casanova. However, as is usual with Patterson's plot structures, this is misleading; Sachs has been deliberately set up by Casanova and The Gentleman Caller, and the real Casanova remains unidentified. Cross works this out, creates a trap, and in the novel's actual crisis kills Casanova, who turns out to have been a detective with the Durham, North Carolina, police, a fine example of the criminal as least likely suspect.

In the denouement, we learn that Gary Soneji has escaped from prison and that a new murder has been committed in Cross's territory; in other words, life returns to its usual pattern for Alex Cross.

CHARACTER DEVELOPMENT

The protagonist of *Kiss the Girls* is Alex Cross and he is both a fully rounded character, in that we have a good deal of information about him, and a dynamic character, in that he changes as a result of his experiences in the novel. Readers who begin the Cross series with the first of these novels, *Along Came a Spider,* may feel that they already know him; however, they will find a much fuller picture of Cross's background and extended family in *Kiss the Girls*, as well as an insightful description of how he sees himself in the world.

In this novel Cross is still a homicide detective with the Washington, D.C. police, and he is still an anomaly in the department given that he has a doctorate in psychology, a rather unusual qualification for a policeman. He continues to mourn for his wife Maria, killed in a drive-by shooting some four years before this story begins. He is a fine father who treasures his seven-year-old son and five-year old daughter, and they in turn clearly treasure him. The three live with Nana Mama, Cross's grandmother and the woman who brought him up after his own parents were killed in an automobile accident when he was nine years old. All of this information is a repetition of the Alex Cross drawn in *Spider.* However, what is new here are the details on Cross's extended family. We learn that of his two brothers, Aaron and Charles, only Charles is still living. Aaron died of cirrhosis of the liver when he was 33. His widow, Cilla, is a good friend to Cross, someone that he has come to like, he says, more than he did his brother. These are tantalizing bits of information that help to fill out Cross's background, and at the same time they leave the reader wondering what exactly the relationship between the three brothers was and why it is that Cross is never shown interacting with the remaining brother, Charles, even in the scene when they are together in Cross's house. Such open-ended descriptions are typical of novels in a series, enticing readers to go on to the next novel in hopes of answering questions raised in earlier ones.

There is also more information about Cross's inner life in this novel. He says that for the last few months he has been having trouble in his life, and later in the novel he tells a character who has become a close friend that he feels empty and screwed up since his wife died (213), and later in the story he tells the same person that he is afraid of forming attachments, "afraid of losing someone I love that much again" (321).

The reader also is given more information in *Kiss the Girls* about Cross's feelings toward his job when he says that he no longer takes a professional attitude toward his work, distancing himself from it as he should, that instead he has come to the point where he takes it personally, even though he knows that this is a sure way to burn out. Such personalizing is heightened here, where one of the victims is his niece, the only child of his dead brother.

There is also new information on Cross as an action hero, particularly in a shoot-out scene in North Carolina where Cross confronts both killers on a busy street filled with drivers and pedestrians and takes out one of the killers, after first commandeering a Plymouth Duster from a tavern parking lot with the classic words, "Police. . . . I have to take your car." The hapless and now car-less civilian driving the Duster says, "Jesus Christ, man. This here's my girlfriend's car" (412), a reaction that feels exactly right—people really do make irrelevant comments when they're startled and under stress. The details that follow describing the chase and shooting are tense and breathtaking, and would be right at home in a Clint Eastwood adventure film.

Information that is not new but that emphasizes earlier background established for Cross is detail on how well known he is as an investigator—the killer Casanova knows exactly who he is, and relishes the challenge of outwitting him. There is also more evidence here of Cross's superb detecting skills. He sees a name buried in reams of back editions of old newspapers and realizes at once that it is key to the solution of the crime. He has been offered a position with the FBI's VICAP (Violent Criminals Apprehension Program) Behavioral Sciences division, an unusual accolade for a policeman, and he is the author of a well-received book on the psychopathic killer, Gary Soneji. All of this establishes that Cross is definitely above the usual run of policemen—when he is part of an investigation, everyone knows that it must be one of significance.

An aspect that adds to this being the fullest description of Alex Cross as a character is his awareness of his color in this novel. In his African American neighborhood in D.C., Cross takes himself and those around him for granted, and any comment he makes on color has to do with the establishment's attitude toward crime in the poorest area of D.C., which also happens to be the African American area. In *Kiss the Girls*, though,

Cross's comments have become personal; he is very aware of himself as an African American who will be working in the American South, and he knows that there, he will be treated as a stereotype rather than as a member of a professional group, and that indeed, in many cases he may well be the first professional African American ever seen in these parts. As the novel nears its conclusion, the North Carolina police come to accept Cross and he thinks, "I was beginning to like it in the South a little, more than I would have thought possible" (422), showing that his attitude has changed and he is now more open to the respect that his abilities can gain him anywhere, with any group of people. It is this new awareness that makes him a dynamic character.

Kiss the Girls has two other protagonists, one familiar to Alex Cross novels, one a new character, and both are drawn with affection and respect. The first of these is John Sampson, Alex Cross's partner in the Washington, D.C., police. When the reader first meets him in *Along Came a Spider,* Sampson is a flat character who exists mainly for Cross to have someone to play off against. In *Kiss the Girls* Sampson, like Cross, is more developed, and it is at least arguable that he has become a dynamic character. He and Cross became best friends when they were both 10 years old; later, when Cross went on to college, Sampson went into the army. Cross says that after this, "In some mysterious manner, we both ended up working together on the DC police force" (29), and canny readers may well expect that this mysterious manner will be described in a later Cross novel. At six foot nine Sampson dwarfs the six-foot-three Cross, and they must make an imposing pair indeed when they walk side by side down any street in America. Sampson is loyal, supportive, and intuitive in his investigative methods as well as in his life; he always seems to know when Cross is in trouble, and the spontaneous questions and comments that he makes regarding on-going investigations help Cross to arrive at final answers. While, in his black leather outfits and Wayfarer sunglasses, he gives the impression of being street-smart only, he is in fact a very well-read man. This particular novel is the only instance in the series of Sampson losing his cool, an event that happens when he and Cross are in North Carolina and are pulled over by the police there solely because they are black. A wonderful confrontation scene follows when Sampson and Cross, in their impressive height, get out of their car and present their police credentials, and following this scene, the extremely reticent Sampson expresses his outrage at being treated in this way. It is this event that makes him into a dynamic character, changing from a distant onlooker to an outraged participant.

An unusual element of the Cross-Sampson relationship is their open acknowledgement of their fondness for one another. Sampson refers to Cross as "Brown Sugar," and they readily tell one another that they love one another, a stance that requires bravado in a world where close male friendships are suspect. Perhaps, with their impressive heights, Sampson and Cross are free to adopt any stance they like without fear of other people's judgments. The relationship also demonstrates their separateness from the police bureaucracy around them and the respect that it shows them, at least in their home police force; these two fine investigators have earned the right to create their own personas.

Patterson's third major protagonist in *Kiss the Girls* is Kate McTiernan, a doctor who is a first-year internist at North Carolina University Hospital. She is a well-developed but static character, in that we know a good deal about her and yet she remains the same person at the end of the novel as she was at the beginning, despite the traumatic experiences she goes through in the story. Like all of Patterson's female protagonists in the Cross series, she is very beautiful, and Kate is the ultimate survivor. She is physically powerful—she holds a black belt in karate—and she is the only one of Casanova's captives to escape from him, something she does purely on the basis of her own efforts and her extraordinary courage. It is because of the information she brings back when she escapes that Cross is ultimately led to Casanova's hideout and the remaining captives are saved. She and Cross share a fear of forming close relationships, Cross because of his wife's death and Kate because of her family history. She is one of five girls, three of whom have died of ovarian or breast cancer. This is also the cause of her mother's death, and she is afraid that it will be her death warrant, too. So far, she has survived this threat, and perhaps it is this that gives her the strength to also survive Casanova; certainly, it sets up for the reader a scenario in which Kate might plausibly triumph over him, even though no one else has done so—she has had much more experience than his other victims at being confronted by death. She and Cross become close friends who decide that they cannot become lovers, that they are too much alike to form a relationship in which they would complement one another. This is a decision that feels exactly right to the reader since it allows Kate to continue on the path she has set for herself, that of going back to her roots in West Virginia where she will work as a doctor in impoverished, rural areas. A testament to Kate's fine character is the fact that the taciturn John Sampson, specialist in a sardonic world view, likes her very much. Sampson is astute and wary and if he approves of Kate, she has to be all right.

The novel's major antagonists are Dr. Will Rudolph, who has named himself "The Gentleman Caller," and Detective Nick Ruskin of the North Carolina police, who has named himself "Casanova." Of these two, Ruskin/Casanova is the dominant personality. There is a great deal of detail on what Casanova thinks of himself, on his capture of women and on how he prepares himself for his crimes, so much so that he appears to be a well-rounded character. However, there is almost no information on his background, so that the reader knows what he does and how he does it but has little insight into why he does it. Cross surmises that Casanova may have been abused as a child and may even have been the victim of incest. However, these speculations remain just that and are never confirmed. Paradoxically, this makes him one of James Patterson's most interesting antagonists—the reader finds him mesmerizing and wants to know more about him, about who he is and how he became the way he is.

One detail that makes Ruskin/Casanova fascinating is his use of body paint; he sees himself as a warrior and he paints his body in vivid colors so that he looks like a savage hunter. He also wears masks of various designs. Cross thinks that the masks represent the different faces of a dark god, the character that Ruskin/Casanova believes himself to be. The descriptions of body paint and masks are some of Patterson's best writing, and they bring to life this basically static character, a man who ends the novel as the same killer he began it. Readers are so gripped by the visual images of Casanova that they are oblivious to what they do not know—the little that is known is simply overwhelming in its sharp imagery.

The other major antagonist is Casanova's friend and sometime-partner, Will Rudolph/The Gentleman Caller. There is a good deal less information on Rudolph than on Casanova. He is a medical doctor, his father was a very strict military man, and he met Casanova when Casanova, as Ruskin, was investigating a homicide committed by Rudolph. It is at this point that the two bond, sharing experiences and emotional highs. The act of doing so is what Cross describes as "twinning," and when Rudolph leaves North Carolina for California, the act represents his attempt to separate himself and establish his independence from Casanova. However, Rudolph is very lonely without him and by novel's end has returned to North Carolina and to the companionship of his fellow psychopath, someone with whom he feels normal. From this perspective he can be seen as a dynamic character, since he goes from attempted independence back to dependence.

There are other minor antagonists such as the pornography-loving professor of philosophy, Dr. Wick Sachs. Such characters serve as red herrings to distract the reader from the true murderers, and as such, they have little significance in their own right; their only function is to make the plot more complex and more puzzling and thus create a better mystery.

SETTING

The use of setting in *Kiss the Girls* is particularly imaginative and adds much to the feel of the novel. One effect of artificial, or man-made, setting is to create a strong image of Alex Cross's Southeast D.C. neighborhood, with its boarded-up stores covered in graffiti, its streets littered with trash and broken liquor bottles. The only natural setting here is that of neglect—a landscape of weeds. As Cross notes, this is indeed a dangerous neighborhood to live in, even for a policeman, and ironically, it is the nation's capital.

A particularly effective combination of artificial and natural settings is the description of the lair where Casanova keeps his captives. In the woods of North Carolina, he has made use of an underground site developed more than 100 years ago to hide runaway slaves, and given its original use, it is certainly believable that this area would be cleverly designed to escape detection. It exists on many levels and Casanova has put electricity and modern amenities into it; this does nothing to make the warren of cells less terrifying, though. It is a multi-level underground dungeon that disappears when one exits it—the surrounding landscape is such that the lair is totally hidden and if it had not been for Kate McTiernan's escape and subsequent information on the site, it is unlikely that any of the women would have been saved. While Patterson has made use of underground settings in the Gary Soneji novels, these are settings that have personal significance for Soneji and it is only by understanding their meaning for him that the reader perceives them as terrifying. However, the underground sites used to hide fugitive slaves are a historical fact and carry with them the ambiance of real-life terror, creating the same claustrophobic sense of horror as do descriptions of the extraordinary places where Nazi victims hid during the Second World War. People, it would seem, cannot live in such places; alternatively, there are circumstances under which such places are their only hope for continuing to live.

POINT OF VIEW

Patterson's point of view in *Kiss the Girls* is consistent with that used in most of the other Alex Cross novels; whenever Cross is the central character in a particular scene, that scene is told from first person or "I" point of view, so that the reader identifies with Cross, knows what he knows, feels what he feels. When events center on other characters such as Casanova and The Gentleman Caller, the point of view switches to third person omniscient so that the reader sees events from the perspective of an unknown narrator who somehow knows all. This is especially useful in a work featuring such bizarre serial killers as Casanova and The Gentleman Caller, who see themselves as simply acting out what they believe to be every man's inner fantasies. Only from the outside is their pathology apparent; viewed from within their own perspectives they are normal, so that if first person were used in the chapters featuring them, the reader would lose the sense of how truly crazed these characters are.

THEMATIC ISSUES

A strong theme in *Kiss the Girls* is that everyone wears a mask of some sort. Of course the most obvious example of this is Casanova, who literally does wear masks, some of them marvelously painted depictions of savage warriors, some of them actual masks used in morgues and mortuaries to form life-like images of the dead. When Casanova uses them, masks are intended to hide his true identity and to create his new identity as a killer and bringer of death; they disguise the fact that he is a policeman, someone sworn to uphold the law and protect others from the death he brings. His psychological twin, The Gentleman Caller, uses as his mask the fact that he dresses like a gentleman and acts as the soul of courtesy, someone anyone could trust on sight. In actual fact he is a voyeur and stalker of women and anything but courteous to them; he kills them and dismembers their corpses for souvenirs. He is specifically aware of his double nature, referring to himself as Dr. Jekyll and Mr. Hyde, from the Robert Louis Stevenson novel (*The Strange Case of Dr. Jekyll and Mr. Hyde*, 1886). When he is in his "normal" mode, The Gentleman Caller thinks of himself as the good Dr. Jekyll; when he is in his killing mode, he thinks of himself as the monstrous Mr. Hyde.

Professor Wick Sachs, a handsome, admired teacher of philosophy and therefore a collector of knowledge, is also wearing a mask; he is a secret collector of pornography, which is hidden in a locked room in his basement. Kate McTiernan, a doctor who is dedicated to saving lives and is justifiably proud of her physical prowess, uses these traits to mask her terror of her own possibly imminent mortality, a mortality based on her family history of cancer. Alex Cross, a psychologist who, like McTiernan, is dedicated to healing others, in his case by helping them to understand their emotional problems, is another example of someone wearing a mask; he says that he himself is an emotional mess, a man scarred by the death of his wife, unable to form new commitments and unable to resolve his own problems. And John Sampson, street-wise, unflappable, and untouchable in his dark glasses and black clothes, turns out to be sensitive and empathetic, someone very much open to others, a sensitivity he disguises by his appearance. Even settings are suspect; a pastoral wooded area disguises the underground cells of a mad kidnapper, and an upper middle-class neighborhood of handsome American-dream homes hides a secret library of pornography. This thematic pattern of distortion through the use of various disguises creates a world in which nothing is what it seems and everything is suspect, a world in which readers must constantly search for clues to character and motivation and where an answer given on page 10 may turn out to be false on page 11. This emphasis on who people really are, as opposed to how they present themselves to the world, adds a good deal to the mystery and uncertainty of *Kiss the Girls;* not until the end are readers confident of knowing the solution to the puzzle, and even then, given Patterson's use of recurring characters, the solution may very well turn out to be temporary, one more mask hiding a reality that will be revealed in a subsequent novel.

ALTERNATIVE READING: THE SOCIOLOGICAL NOVEL

As noted in Chapter 4, a sociological novel "concentrates on the nature, function and effect of the society in which characters live" (Holman and Harmon 1992, 448). It includes within it the serious consideration of issues current in the society—sometimes with the goal of correcting them in specific ways, at other times simply with the goal of exposing them. Classic sociological novels are Harriet Beecher Stowe's *Uncle Tom's Cabin* (1852), with its deeply moving portrait of slaves in pre-Civil War America; Charles Dickens's *Hard Times* (1854) with its vivid descriptions of the plight of the working class in Victorian England; and John Steinbeck's *The Grapes of Wrath* (1939), with its wrenching portrayal of Oklahomans who emigrated to California because of the ravages of the Dust Bowl.

James Patterson has previously made use of the novel to make sociological comments in *Along Came a Spider,* where he focuses primarily on large issues affecting a group as a whole, such as the establishment's attitudes toward crime in the ghetto. In *Kiss the Girls,* Patterson alters his focus slightly, giving a sharp, painful picture of how any individual African American can expect to be discriminated against at any time, in any circumstances. He does this in a powerful scene in which Cross and Sampson are at a stop sign in Chapel Hill, North Carolina, and suddenly a Smith and Wesson revolver is pointed directly into Cross's face. "Chapel Hill police!" a man shouts. "Get the hell out of the car. Assume the position" (332). Both men are very aware of the danger that they're in, with the ever-cool Sampson telling Alex not to get them shot up. They have, of course, done nothing wrong; they're just African Americans stopped at a stop sign at ten o'clock in the morning in a large American city. They get out of the car, and are attacked before they can even identify themselves. This would make a superb film scene, with the six-foot-three and six-foot-nine D.C. policemen under attack. Cross shouts out that he is a policeman on the Casanova case and, at the same time, floors the policeman attacking him. Sampson, usually so quiet and contained, screams, "How many brothers you pull that shit on? How many young men you call 'homes' and humiliate like that?—like you might fuckin' understand what their life is about. Makes me sick" (335). It makes the reader sick too, since it so obviously rings true—this is what racial profiling is all about, and even the police themselves are not immune from being targets of it, not if they are African American.

Other less dramatic but just as pointed sociological statements are scattered throughout the novel, most of them commenting on living conditions for all African Americans in poor neighborhoods rather than on Cross in particular. At the beginning of the novel, when Cross is rushing the boy who has attempted suicide to the hospital, running down the street with him in his arms, an E.M.S. ambulance goes by him without stopping or even slowing down and Cross is not surprised: he says that life in that neighborhood is like that, that "you can't stop for every murder or mugging that you come across on your daily rounds" (21). Once he has the child in the emergency room, he shouts for help and is ignored, and he thinks that even a pizza delivery man would have gotten more attention. In this case, Cross is in an African American setting, emphasizing that this is what life is like for African Americans in contemporary urban America. They are suspect on the basis of their color alone, attacked for that reason, and all too often ignored by other African Americans, who are themselves overwhelmed with their own problems. As in *Along Came a Spider,* Patterson has no solutions to pose. Instead, he continues to focus on exposing the flaws in the society, flaws that must as a first step be recognized before we can begin to formulate remedies.

6

Jack & Jill (1996)

With *Jack & Jill* James Patterson returns to a topic he introduced 20 years earlier in *The Thomas Berryman Number*, that of the assassination of a charismatic political figure that has been ordered by members of a conservative conspiracy. In *The Thomas Berryman Number* the victim is Jimmie Horn, a Martin Luther King, Jr.-like mayor of a Southern city, and in *Jack & Jill* it is Thomas Byrnes, a John F. Kennedy-like President of the United States. Assassination is clearly a topic that continues to fascinate Patterson and perhaps one that he finds more and more perplexing as time goes on. In *The Thomas Berryman Number* the reader leaves the novel certain of who the man behind the killing was and of his motivation for the murder, whereas in *Jack & Jill*, whoever is the mastermind of the assassination is never identified and the suggestion is that he or she (or possibly a group) continues to exist, unidentified and unapprehended, ready to plan and implement future political assassinations.

GENRE

In terms of its genre, Patterson continues the pattern he has established in the first two Alex Cross novels, that of crossing the police procedural with the romance and the sociological novel (see Chapter 2 for a detailed discussion of these genres). Once again, Patterson follows the conventions of the procedural by having the crimes be solved by detectives going about the usual routines of their daily lives, rather than by the brilliant intuitive leaps of amateurs such as Sherlock Holmes. He also focuses on the hardships of being a policeman: the low pay, the long hours, and the disruptions to family life. Another frequent element of the procedural is the antagonism between the working detectives and their superiors; while the police seek to contain crime, it often seems to them that their superiors are seeking to create good public relations to ensure their own survival, so that certain cases involving high-profile citizens receive far more attention than similar cases involving the poor. This is a strong theme in *Jack & Jill,* where Cross's superior officer is hostile to him and obstructive to his work.

One area in which Patterson breaks with tradition is in his depiction of the interaction of the Washington, D.C., police, the FBI, and the Secret Service. Typically these separate branches of law enforcement are drawn as rivals who are in competition with one another to find answers, and who jealously hide information from one another in order to be first at a solution. In *Jack & Jill,* however, all agencies cooperate, perhaps to underlie the seriousness of the threat presented by the killers—this is one case where groups cannot afford to compete because so much is at stake here (ultimately, the life of the President).

Another atypical aspect of *Jack & Jill* is its inclusion of what could be considered a vigilante group within the ranks of the police itself. This is made up of Cross and four of his friends from the D.C. detective squad, all of them African American and all of them living in Southeast, one of D.C.'s poorest areas. They have come together to continue the investigation of what has become two murders of children in their neighborhood, since the police assigned to the case have now been pulled off it to focus instead on the high profile murders of celebrities by Jack and Jill. First introduced in this novel, the vigilante group will continue to act in *Cat & Mouse* and *Pop! Goes the Weasel.* In doing so it pre-figures a similar group in Patterson's later, non-Cross series, *1st to Die* and *2nd Chance.*

While it is highly unlikely that such a vigilante group would exist within a real-life police force, it is a very effective device for reinforcing Patterson's continuing use of the Cross novels as sociological statements that make strong comments on the conditions in which the poor and black in the nation's capitol live, and the attitude of the establishment toward these conditions. At the beginning of the novel, a killer on the prowl for his next victim is pleased that nearly all the potential targets around him are African American. He sees them as safe targets, since "Nobody gave a damn about the blacks in D.C. That was a fact of life" (8). One of the deaths in *Jack & Jill* is that of a five-year-old girl, of whom Cross says, "In most cities, in most civilized countries, a child murdered so young would be a catastrophe, but not in Washington, where hundreds of children die violent deaths every single year" (32–33). Overall, Patterson draws a picture of a city whose poor neighborhoods are abandoned by man and by God, areas where nothing much works and where no one cares.

Finally, as a romance novel, *Jack & Jill* continues Patterson's use of a strong love story as part of the overall plot, introducing here the character of Christine Johnson, a continuing character in the two Cross novels following this one, *Cat & Mouse* and *Pop! Goes the Weasel.*

PLOT DEVELOPMENT

In *Jack & Jill,* James Patterson once again begins with a prologue to set the tone of the novel and to introduce his primary antagonists, Jack and Jill. As the novel opens, Jack is thinking about horror stories, comparing the ones children tell around campfires to play the game of scaring themselves, something that they recognize is indeed a game, with "the real-life horror stories that are around us everywhere these days" (5). He himself, he says, is about to become part of the horror, and here Patterson, who has both a Bachelor's and a Master's degree in English, is calling up echoes of Joseph Conrad's short story "The Heart of Darkness" (1902), in which a cultured, educated European goes to the then-Belgian Congo and descends into savagery, a story famous for its ability to terrify the reader with the possibility that each of us lives on the edge and that it is frighteningly easy to move "past the edge and into the darkness" (5). Jack is stalking a senator in order to murder him, something that he refers to as part of the game. The effect of the prologue, then, is that the reader is alerted to a novel that will presumably deal with savagery enacted as some form of game, although the game's purpose is unidentified.

The second chapter introduces another creature of horror, a murderer attempting to lure a child to him so that he can kill her. He too uses aspects of a game to do this, enticing her with brightly colored balloons that she can choose from, and the murder he commits is indeed savage; he crushes her skull with an aluminum baseball bat, a weapon that is itself connected with a game. The novel now continues to shift back and forth between these two antagonists, setting up a series of contrasts between them: one murderer is a highly intelligent and well-respected adult, the other is an equally intelligent but troubled youngster for whom others seem to have little regard; one has received extensive military training, the other is a student in a military academy; one kills adult celebrities, the other kills poor, unknown children; one leaves poems with the victim, the other leaves e-mail messages on Prodigy; and ultimately, one ends up jailed and then dead while the other presumably will receive treatment for his mental demons.

Once the prologue has established the novel's parameters, the original situation opens with Alex Cross assigned to the murder of a child in Southeast. He goes about a typical police investigation, examining the scene of the crime, questioning witnesses, and canvassing the neighborhood. He believes that he has found the killer, a bizarre creature known as Chop-it Off Chucky, who jumps to his death in attempting to escape Cross. The novel's first major complication occurs when, after the death of Chucky, a second child is murdered in exactly the same manner as the first and it is apparent that the murderer is still free. Simultaneous with the children's murders, a senator is murdered in a hotel in downtown Washington, D.C., possibly by a psychopath since the body is horribly mutilated. Cross is removed from the child murder case and assigned to the senator's case; as a psychologist Cross has experience with psychopaths, and the death of the senator is considered far more important than the death of two African American children from the ghetto. He continues, though, to investigate the death of the children on his own, and the two series of murders continue to unfold, with the killers in each continuing to plot and execute additional killings.

Jack and Jill's crimes are by far the most dramatic of the two plot lines, since they choose prominent, nationally known figures as their victims: a senator, a newswoman, an actor, and a law student who, it turns out, is having an affair with a Supreme Court justice, and who may have been killed by accident, the justice being the intended victim. Jack and Jill's ultimate goal is to assassinate the President of the United States who, confusingly, is then assassinated by another killer (this is reminiscent of *The Thomas Berryman Number,* with its uncertainty over who killed Jimmie Horn). The goal of the child killer is to achieve some sort of internal peace, even though he knows that he cannot do so by the means he is using. Nonetheless, as with Jack and Jill, he continues his killing.

The climax of a mystery is usually the identification of the killer and Patterson accomplishes this with his customary misdirection of readers, who are led to think that they know the killer, only to discover that they have been misled. Thus, the child murderer turns out to be little more than a child himself and not the deviant Chucky, and Jack turns out not to be working with Jill, a tool whom he kills when she ceases to be useful, but with his wife, the inspector general of the C.I.A.

In the denouement, readers are given no information about what will ultimately happen to the child killer. However, the fate of Jack and Jill is in no doubt; both are found dead in their prison cells. If the deaths were suicides, someone had to get to them and supply them with the means. If they were murders, again, someone had to get to them, and do so inside a closely guarded federal prison. Cross believes that they were murdered to keep them quiet so that they could not expose the mastermind behind the presidential assassination. Who murdered them is a question that remains unanswered, so that although their fates are known, the agent of those fates remains unidentified. In the final scene, Alex Cross receives a phone call from Gary Soneji, the psychopath introduced in the first Cross novel, *Along Came a Spider.* Soneji has escaped from prison and wants Cross to know, "Gary's real close!" (466). Thus, there is no closure to *Jack & Jill,* suggesting that it is ultimately impossible to eradicate evil, that the horror will always be with us.

CHARACTER DEVELOPMENT

As in all of Patterson's Alex Cross novels, Alex Cross is the central character and the protagonist or hero. He is a well-rounded character, someone of whom we are given much information. In this particular novel his family life is lightly sketched in, although he remains the loving father Patterson first introduced in *Along Came a Spider,* devoting as much time as his job will allow to his two young children, Damon and Jannie, who have a warm, teasing relationship with him and thoroughly enjoy the time they are able to spend with him, limited as it is by the constraints of his job. The family still lives with Nana Mama, Cross's now 81-year-old grandmother, who acts as both mother and grandmother to the three Crosses. As with his family life, Cross's personal relationships are also lightly drawn here. John Sampson remains his best friend as well as his partner on the Washington, D.C., police force, although Sampson's role in the novel is minor and he seems to be here for consistency in the series rather than for plot necessity. Cross's love interest in this novel is also underemphasized since it is a case of nascent romance. Here, he is very attracted to a lovely woman, principal of his son's school, who is, when he meets her, married to someone else; however, the attraction remains unresolved in the pages of this story (it will be resolved in later works).

In terms of Cross as a character, the emphasis in *Jack & Jill* is on his professional skills. He is a good street detective, which he demonstrates by his ability to analyze crime scenes and put together clues, something he impressively does in the opening murder of the child and then again in his quick, intuitive reading of Jack and Jill's murders, where he recognizes before anyone else that their killings take the form of a game. He is highly regarded by his peers, even those in other law enforcement agencies. The FBI formally requests Cross's help on the Jack and Jill case because of his experience with psychopathic killers, and this is followed by the Secret Service's request that Cross assist in solving the murders—something rather out of the ordinary for the typical street detective and, as noted earlier, an aberration in the police procedural genre, where different branches jealously guard their jurisdictions.

Cross's method of working is essentially Socratic, in that he asks himself a series of questions, ones that he continually adds to, and the implication is that the very act of asking the question helps him to arrive at an answer. On the second Jack and Jill killing, Cross isolates, as needing answers, how the killers choose their victims, whether the killings are part of a sexual bond between them, if this is step one in a multiple crime spree, if it will spread to other major cities, why the killers want to create the illusion that kinky sex is an aspect of the deaths, the possibility that Jack is impotent, and, given Cross's conclusion that one of the killers is an artist, what sort of artist would become a participant in such killings. He uses the same self-questioning technique in his investigation of the child murders in Southeast, an authorial device that works to allow the reader to become a detective along with Cross: we know what he's thinking and what the important questions are, and therefore, we too might be able to arrive at a solution.

In attempting to arrive at answers to his questions, Cross tells himself, "*Think like the killer. Walk in the killer's shoes*" (182; italics in original). He does this through education and practice. As a psychologist with a Ph.D. from Johns Hopkins University, Cross is adept at analyzing personalities—that is, at thinking as others might—and he combines this background in his role as a detective with a compulsive attention to detail that will help him envision those personalities. However, if Cross is clearly valued in his professional life, esteemed by his colleagues, and sure in his ability to fill this role, in his private life he craves approval that he can never receive and suffers from a feeling of abandonment that he is afraid cannot be overcome. He tells his analyst, "I suspect that I still want to please my mother and father. . . . Sometimes I feel that both my parents died of a kind of terminal sadness, and that my brothers and I were part of their sorrow. I'm afraid that I have it, too" (227). Certainly he is entitled to feel a great sense of loss, since in addition to his parents' early deaths he has also lost his beloved wife in a senseless shooting. However, this novel is the first time that Cross has articulated his feelings, especially those of seeking an approval that can never be received.

In terms of Cross's status as a static (unchanging) or dynamic (evolving) character, Patterson, who typically has Cross begin each novel as essentially the same person that he ends it, varies this in *Jack & Jill* and makes of his usually static character an evolving one. At the beginning of the novel, Cross is seriously considering leaving the police force and returning to private practice as a psychologist. He reacts personally to crimes, and this is becoming more and more something that he cannot handle, something, he says, that eats at him "like acid splashed all over my body" (27). However, his attitude changes as the story progresses, so that by a quarter of the way through he says that he is hooked on the Jack and Jill case and although, only a few pages later, he cannot answer the question of why he does the kind of work that he does, by the novel's end he has come to recognize that leaving the police would be another loss for him, and with this realization, he has accepted his profession. He thinks back to himself as a child who wondered what he would become as a grown-up and he says that now he knows; he is "a multiple-homicide expert who got to work the biggest, nastiest cases" (419). Thus he has gone from being a man on the verge of leaving the police to being a man who accepts his role as an expert in a very unsavory aspect of human existence, and his term for himself, "Dragonslayer," carries with it implications of duty, of the knight who must as part of his identity slay the dragons who threaten innocents in the society he lives in.

Other positive characters in *Jack & Jill* are John Sampson, Cross's partner and friend since childhood, Nana Mama, Cross's group of four African American detectives who, as noted, act as a private crime-fighting group within the police force, Christine Johnson, the married woman Cross is strongly attracted to in this story, and various F.B.I. and Secret Service operatives who are working on the case. Of these only Sampson is described in any detail; we know how he dresses (usually in black leather with black Wayfarers), Cross's nickname for him (Man Mountain, in honor of Sampson's six-foot-nine height), that he is well-read (he is currently reading Camus), that he looks like a Masai warrior, and that one of his deepest secrets is that he cannot bear the sight of decomposing bodies. All of these minor protagonists are static, ending the novel as they have begun it.

In terms of antagonists or villains, in Danny Boudreaux, a 13-year-old who is very disturbed, Patterson has created what is his only sympathetic killer to date. Danny has murdered four people, two young children, a schoolmate, and the husband of Christine Johnson, and yet the reader aches for him. He is seriously disturbed, and despite the fact that he is an adolescent, he comes across to the reader as a child—he is only five foot three inches, and at 120 pounds, he makes little in the way of a physical impression. When he kills, tears stream down his face. He is either suffering from bipolar disorder or conduct disorder—his doctors cannot agree. Just before his killings begin he has stopped taking his medication, although no reason is given for this. He hates himself and is suicidal, only waiting for someone else to perform the action of killing him. When Cross meets up with him he thinks, "I doubted that anyone had ever liked Danny Boudreaux too much. I didn't" (405). Cross sees him as being like Gary Soneji, the antagonist of *Along Came a Spider* and *Cat & Mouse*, and it does indeed seem more than likely that if Boudreaux is left to develop as he is going, he will end up another Soneji, another highly imaginative murderer of children. Nonetheless, it is difficult not to feel sorry for Boudreaux. His mother is dead and his father has abandoned him, and he has spent most of his life in foster care. When Cross apprehends him, Boudreaux tells him, "I'm afraid. . . . I'm always so afraid" (415), and the statement has the ring of truth. He is a relatively rounded character, since the reader knows at least some of his background and what his motives for the killings are. On the other hand, he is a static character, ending the novel as the killer he was when it began.

The antagonists in the second plot thread, the Jack and Jill murders, are Sam Harrison, who is the dominant figure, his lover Sara Rosen, and three surprise antagonists, Kevin Hawkins, Jeanne Sterling, and, in a cameo appearance, Chief of Detectives Pittman. Of these, by far the most important is Sam Harrison, who plays the role of Jack in the killings. He is a tall, handsome man code-named "The Soldier" by whoever has masterminded the series of killings, a code name that suggests he is only following orders, although we never learn the source of these orders. He has been assigned to work with Jill, although whoever is doing the assigning remains unidentified. Harrison is the most developed of the antagonists in this second plot and Cross sees him as involved in some sort of private war to restore his—or his group's—vision of America. He has great personal charm and magnetism, and Jill falls in love with him as soon as she meets him. Cross believes that he may well be a CIA agent who has become a rogue, that is, someone who is acting outside the confines of the agency and is using the trade-craft he has learned there to accomplish his personal ends. Harrison thinks of his murders as executions, although, again, why his victims deserve to be executed is left unanswered. At other times he envisions himself as fighting a war, and while he has occasional glimmers that his is not normal, that he is a sick man, he is able to immediately shut down these thoughts by forcing himself to focus on his task. The Harrison introduced here is Harrison as he is now, after he has become Jack the Assassin. How he came to this point is never explored, and, when he kills Jill, whom he genuinely seems to love, there is an abrupt discontinuity for the reader. The Harrison presented turns out to be not at all as he has been drawn, and the crimes that initially were described as being organized by Harrison, with Jill's help, have in reality been organized by someone else entirely, with Harrison acting as that person's agent, someone whose identity is never made known. At the very end of the novel, when it develops that Harrison is actually Brett Sterling and that he is married to yet another Jill, he is poisoned, presumably by his anonymous controller, whom we assume to be the primary conspirator in this series of killings. Thus, we know a good deal about Harrison's surface personality and very little about what and who drives him. This surface personality is compelling enough to make him a developed figure, although he remains static throughout, a firm believer in his role as a righteous killer.

Harrison's partner, Jill, is Sara Rosen, a bright, intelligent, articulate member of the White House staff. She and Harrison have been put in touch with one another by an unnamed outsider, presumably the person directing the assassinations. Rosen is a very attractive woman who walks with a slight limp, and she has, before meeting Harrison, defined herself in terms of the limp. His attraction for her is that he changes her perception of herself so that she can become something other than a cripple. We know less about her than we do about Harrison—there are fewer details to fill in since she is not married, has no children, and why she has joined this killing conspiracy is never clarified. All we know is that, like Harrison, she sees it as her patriotic duty. She is so much in love with Harrison that it is difficult to separate this as a motivator from her ideological stance, one that is never explored. When, at the end of the novel, she is killed by him, she seems to have no anticipation that this might happen to her, suggesting that she is rather naïve, despite her role in the killings. She is a static character, believing in her mission and in Jack/Harrison until the end.

A third antagonist is a photojournalist named Kevin Hawkins. At 43 years old, he feels more like 100—he has lived a hard, fast life. Now he is in Washington to assassinate the president, although his action seems coincidental to Jack and Jill's plot, since Hawkins is a right-wing extremist who is known for acting on his own. Ultimately, Patterson leaves it unclear as to the true assassin; from the development of the story it could be either Sam Harrison or Kevin Hawkins, each of whom is on the site and each of whom is armed. In terms of Hawkins as a character, he is only sketched in, a burned-out, fast-living man, and the reasons for his extreme patriotism and his determination to kill the president are undeveloped. Given the little the reader knows of him, Hawkins remains a flat, static character, although an intriguing one.

A surprise antagonist is Jeanne Sterling, the first woman to hold the position of Inspector General of the CIA. She is married to Harrison, and it is only at the end of the novel that we learn that she, too, is involved in the assassination plot, that she is the original Jill behind the killings, with Sara Rosen being only a tool that this Jill and her husband used to accomplish their ends. While it is obvious that Sterling is intelligent and capable, given her CIA position, the reader knows very little about her. The assassination plot obviously matters a great deal to her, since she is willing to risk her child's life to protect it, but her motivation is missing; we have no idea how she came to this point, of the person she may once have been as opposed to the person she has become, and so she remains both a flat and a static character throughout the novel, someone whose sole function appears to be that of adding to the ultimately unsolved mystery of what exactly this game is, what its goals are, and who has planned it.

The final antagonist is Alex Cross's immediate superior, Chief of Detectives Pittman. As discussed in Chapter 2, it is a commonplace of the police procedural that superior officers are far more interested in their own reputations and promotions than they are in controlling crime, and Pittman nicely fills this role. This makes him into a stock character, a flat, static character who has become a convention in certain forms of literature. Typical examples are the wicked witch, the cruel stepmother, the femme fatale, the jock lacking in brain power, and so on. In the Cross series, Chief Pittman is drawn as a "bully and . . . a closet racist" (71). He is condescending and patronizing to Cross because he is jealous of him and is afraid that his recognized abilities as a detective will outshine Pittman's own. Pittman is also afraid that Cross is after his job, although he has no evidence that this is so—it is just part of his general envy and distrust of Cross. He is a spiritually ugly man and when he, in an astounding scene that is absolutely out of the ordinary for anyone in a supervisory position, pushes Cross hard with the heel of his hand in what is clearly meant as an assault, Cross immediately thinks of him, "He resents the hell out of me because I'm decent at what I do" (103). Cross, in an equally extraordinary action, fights back, picking Pittman up and slamming him against a wall. All of this happens in the presence of a witness and the fact that Cross gets away with this attack on a superior officer, even though it is in reaction to an attack on himself, speaks to how good Cross is as a detective and to his excellent reputation among other lawmakers—he is, in effect, above the normal rules that apply in the police force. Pittman's animosity toward Cross, his lust for recognition, and his indifference to crime in poor areas is all we learn about him—how he came to be this way or how, indeed, he became Chief of Detectives is unexplored, leaving him a classic example of the stock or one-dimensional character.

SETTING

Throughout the Cross series, Patterson remains fascinated by the discrepancy between the two Washingtons: the powerful world of politics and high finance epitomized by the Capitol buildings and the embassies and the elegant hotels serving them, and the powerless world of drugs and poverty epitomized by the Southeast and Northfield Village housing projects. These two contrasting settings mirror the two plot lines in *Jack & Jill*, with its murders of the rich and powerful contrasted to its murders of the poor and powerless. The former killings take place in apartments with breathtaking views and glamorous concert halls made even more glamorous by their audiences. The latter take place in neighborhoods made up of run-down, deteriorating buildings that look to be on the verge of collapse. It is because of this Southeast/Northfield setting that the killings of children here receive such cursory investigation; they happen in one of the most crime-ridden areas in the city and Cross says that "The 1st District police have given up. You visit Northfield once, it's hard to blame them completely" (50). There is, though, one pastoral location in this artificial setting of decay and neglect, that of the Sojourner Truth School, the neighborhood elementary school. It is "festive, very bright, imaginatively decorated" and Cross thinks that it is a "terrific habitat," a "sweet place" for his son Damon "to grow and to learn" (132).

There is little use of natural setting in the killings committed by Jack and Jill, since these take place in buildings, hotels, concert halls, and the like. However, the child killings committed by Daniel Boudreaux are superbly set, creating a scene that could be straight out of a Grimm's brothers fairy tale. He lures his victims into a wooded bower with overhanging tree branches, a place that makes them feel safe because it is contained and sheltered, and at the same time it hides the killer from sight while he commits his crimes. The reader wants to scream out to the children, "Don't go in the woods!! Don't go in the woods!!" but they are too young to know about Hansel and Gretel and are seduced by the seeming protection of nature.

POINT OF VIEW

As has been noted, Patterson typically uses multiple points of view in his Alex Cross novels, with those chapters focusing on Cross told in first person, from the "I" point of view, and those focusing on the killers told in third person omniscient, in which an unidentified narrator who knows everything takes over the telling of the story. There are many advantages to using these two points of view; when in first person with Alex Cross, the reader knows what is he doing, what he is thinking, what he is wondering. Only in his point of view can the reader be privy to the questions he asks himself that will ultimately lead him to solutions, and because the reader shares the point of view, the reader, too, can ask the questions and hope to come to valid conclusions. In this way, the reader can play detective along with Cross. There is also a more unusual use of first person point of view toward the end of the novel, when Patterson uses it to create a framework narrative, a technique in which a first person narrator tells a story within the primary story being told. In this technique, the narrator acts as a reporter, telling the reader what has happened in another story. Joseph Conrad (1857–1924) made superb use of this technique in many of his stories, creating a narrator named Marlow who, using the "I" voice, tells stories about others that he has learned in his experiences as a sailor. As noted before, Conrad is the source of Patterson's use of the term "the horror," and Holman and Harmon say that Conrad sometimes carried the framework technique "to three or four degrees of quotation as the nameless narrator tells what a story-telling character . . . tells about what other characters say, and so forth." They also list Mary Shelley's *Frankenstein* (1818) as a prime example of the frame tale "because the story of Victor Frankenstein and his monster-creature is included in Robert Walton's account of his northward explorations, related in letters to his sister" (1992, 205).

Whether or not Patterson has been influenced by Conrad in his use of this point of view, up to this point in *Jack & Jill* he has had Cross tell the story as it is unfolding, in strict chronological order. In Chapter 78, though, Cross is reflecting back on it, saying, "There have been many conflicting accounts, but this is what happened and how it happened. I know, because I was there" (329), and the reader is left adrift: is the story over, then? When did it end? Who committed the killings and why? And how does Cross already know? This subtle shift in first person adds to the puzzle aspect of the novel, creating questions beyond the simple ones of how will Jack and Jill and Daniel Boudreaux be stopped. It also adds credibility to the story as a whole, since now we have a first person witness, looking back at leisure and commenting on what has previously happened.

As to Patterson's use of third person omniscient, this performs its usual role of allowing readers to have access to information that would otherwise be unavailable if they had to depend solely on Cross's knowledge, such as how Harrison and Rosen feel about each other and about their victims and the details about Rosen's identification of herself in terms of her limp. It also allows the reader to enter Daniel Boudreaux's mind and see how terribly disturbed he is; through this point of view, the reader is able to feel deeply sorry for a vicious killer, a reaction that is reinforced when Patterson reveals that Boudreaux is only 13 years old.

THEMATIC ISSUES

A basic theme of *Jack & Jill* is that there are no final answers and that the truth eludes us. This is in contrast to the usual convention of mystery and detective fiction where, at the end, all questions are answered, motivations are revealed, patterns of detection are explained, the criminals are brought to justice, and evil, at least in this particular form, is removed from the fictional world of the story. This pattern is essentially an optimistic one, since it assumes that there are answers and that human beings are capable of finding them, if only they are committed to the search for the truth. Such is not the case in *Jack & Jill,* though. No one could be more committed than Alex Cross and yet, at the end, even he is left wondering who is responsible for masterminding the killings.

Uncertainties are introduced at the very beginning of the story, where the antagonist is introduced as Sam Harrison, and then we are immediately told, *"His name wasn't really Sam. Or Harrison"* (5; italics in original). He is wearing glasses, but then we learn that he never wore glasses. He has light blond hair, but we're told that he wasn't really blond. This series of deceptions that remain unresolved (What is his name? Why is he wearing glasses? What color is his hair?) sets up a pattern of questions that causes the reader to continue reading in order to arrive at answers. However, it also sets up a pattern in which answers are held back or are so general as to be non-answers. Thus, Jack and Jill explain in a video that they are assassinating their victims because unscrupulous people have taken over the government and its institutions and the system no longer works. The specifics of this take-over are left unidentified, and exactly what it is that no longer works is left up to the reader to decide. We also do not know how Jack and Jill came to this perception, nor how they see their actions as improving the system or making a basic difference. Jill says of the two of them that they are in a war for survival, "the most important war of our times" (155), and she emphasizes that they both believe this. The exact nature of this war is never explained, nor do we know what the trigger was that brought them to this conclusion. Given that they are both highly intelligent, articulate people who have made careers of working for the government, why do they now find it so dysfunctional? What has convinced them that killings will restore function to the system? These are questions that are posed and then left open, suggesting that they are without answers, that they are simply observations the reader must take as being true on their face.

The theme of uncertainty and impossibility of knowing is repeated in Alex Cross's observations of the FBI and the CIA, both of which he sees as obsessed by conspiracy theories that ultimately have no core, no final solution. And while he is skeptical of these theories, he gives them validity by saying, *"thirty years after the Kennedy assassinations, no one was really convinced that either of those murders had been solved"* (355; italics in original). Later, he observes that he finds it unbelievable that there is no accepted consensus on the solution of two of the three major murder cases of the twentieth century, those of John F. Kennedy and Martin Luther King, Jr. When at the end of the novel Sam Harrison, now no longer Jack, thinks, "In truth, our history was *not knowing;* it was being carefully shielded from the truth. That was the American way" (381), it is clear that he is being candid in his description of how he sees the world and also clear that he has no answers for how we have arrived at where we are, nor for how we might change that. Although he seems to think his actions will make a difference, he never explains why that might be so. The reader is caught in a tautology; if conspiracies have destroyed the fabric of our society, how will the conspiracy of Jack and Jill restore it? The ultimate answer—or non-answer—is that it will not. Jack and Jill themselves die as part of what is more than likely a conspiracy, and the agent of their deaths remains unknown.

This is a most pessimistic ending in a genre that normally ends with the comforting illusion that there are answers and solutions and that, one way or another, evildoers will be brought to justice. In *Jack & Jill*, we don't even know who the evildoers are, and therefore, there is no hope of achieving justice. One of Cross's final comments on the *Jack & Jill* case is that he doubts that anything will ever be all right again (in context, it is clear that he is referring to life in the United States) because *"There are no rules anymore"* (453; italics in original), and without rules, there is no framework for justice. He clings to the notion that if this is true of the society as a whole, he can still have order and logic within his own small domestic world, but this too is exposed as a fantasy when Gary Soneji, the psychopathic killer that Cross captured in *Along Came a Spider* and who has since escaped from prison, calls him at his home to let him know that he's thinking of him, making the point that Soneji is still out there, prowling the world. In this novel there is no ultimate resolution to the Soneji case, the Jack and Jill case, or the Danny Boudreaux case. These are all cases that Cross has worked on, and Cross is one of the best; if he cannot find answers, no one can.

ALTERNATIVE READING: A DYSTOPIA

The term "dystopia" takes its meaning from the term "utopia," one that in literature refers to a place or society where all is well. British author and critic J. A. Cuddon notes that the concept of such a place is of great antiquity, first introduced by Sir Thomas More in 1516 when he named his imaginary republic "Utopia." Cuddon goes on to say, "The seeming impossibility of utopia . . . has created its converse: dystopia or anti-utopia" (1991, 1018) or, literally, a place or society where all is unwell. Classic examples of dystopias are George Orwell's *1984* (1949) and Aldous Huxley's *Brave New World* (1932). Like these novels, the worldview of *Jack & Jill* is so bleak as to put it in the subgenre of dystopia.

This bleakness is immediately apparent in the novel's descriptions of the poorest areas of Washington, D.C. However, it is also apparent in the richest areas of the city too, places that are the sites of elegant homes and, one would assume, the good life. Instead, these are the residences of traitors and murderers, of not only Jack and Jill but of Jeanne Sterling, the CIA Inspector General charged with the protection of the president she conspires to assassinate. Similarly, an elegant penthouse apartment is a sordid one-night-stand retreat for a prominent television newscaster, and an exclusive downtown hotel is the site for a well-known senator's drunken assignations. This makes of Washington a place where there is no good life; in all of its neighborhoods, moral corruption is the norm. It is particularly ironic that this is the nation's capital, the place that should be the showcase of life in America.

An even more disturbing element of dystopia in this novel is the lives of children. Here, what should be the innocent games of childhood are used to lure children to their deaths, children murder other children, and children are betrayed by their parents, by those who should protect and guard them.

Patterson's use of games and game motifs is striking in this novel, and applies to both adults and children. The title, of course, refers to a nursery rhyme, but on close examination it is not a particularly happy one, since it culminates in injuries to the two children in the rhyme, with Jill falling down and breaking her crown (her head), and Jack falling after her. Continuing the theme of games, Sam Harrison and Sarah Rosen choose their victims by means of a board game, throwing dice and counting out their moves to see who they will land on as their next candidate for execution. Danny Boudreaux, the murderer of the children, creates a fort that seems like a safe haven for a child to play in and decorates it with balloons to lure them into it so that he can bludgeon them to death. He himself wears disguises, mimicking the game of dress-up. Alex Cross also contributes to the game motif when he sees Jack and Jill as bizarre psychopaths who are playing a pathological game. At one point, he refers to their being in D.C. as the circus being in town, and of course circuses are associated with childhood and its special treats. Finally, the children's chain toy store, Toys 'R' Us, is the site of a failed abduction of a five-year-old boy by the child murderer Boudreaux, and the reader thinks, "Oh yes, of course. For anyone seeking child victims, a toy store would be a most logical place to hunt," so that what is usually thought of as a magical place of access to the world of play has become a very dangerous place indeed.

In terms of children murdering other children, Danny Boudreaux is still on the borderline of childhood and adolescence since he is only 13 years old, and it is emphasized that he is small and slight for his age and so it is likely that he would create the impression of childhood more than he would of adolescence. And in terms of parental betrayal, whether intended or not, Boudreaux's first victim, six-year-old Shanelle Green, is vulnerable because there is no one watching out for her; her parents must both work to support the family, and although they dearly love the child, love is not enough to safeguard a child in this world. Boudreaux also almost succeeds in taking a five-year-old boy out of a toy store because the child's father has become absorbed in the toys and is paying no attention to the child himself; it is the mother who rescues him from Boudreaux. It would be a mistake, though, to see this as a sign that mothers are the saviors of children, since Jeanne Sterling is willing to sacrifice her youngest child in an escape attempt—the conspiracy and its success are more important to her than the life of her daughter.

Overall, then, in *Jack & Jill* Patterson has created a contemporary dystopia, a bad place where no one is safe, no one is protected, no innocence remains, and he has heightened its bleakness by setting it in the iconic capital of the United States, suggesting, at least in this novel, that there is little hope of living the good life in America.

7

Cat & Mouse (1997)

Cat & Mouse is James Patterson's fourth Alex Cross novel and features many of the same characters who appeared in *Along Came a Spider,* the first of the Cross series. Like that novel, it is a police procedural that makes excellent use of Patterson's background in the mental health field, and also like that novel, it highlights the same protagonist (Alex Cross, the Washington, D.C., homicide detective) and antagonist (Gary Murphy/ Soneji, psychopath and possible multiple personality). *Cat & Mouse* differs from *Along Came a Spider,* however, in its development of these two central characters and in its addition of a second primary plot, one that takes over after the first would seem to have reached its climax. In fact, *Cat & Mouse* could well be described as two novels in one.

GENRE

In terms of genre, *Cat & Mouse* follows the mix of genres Patterson established in its prequel, *Along Came a Spider.* Once again, he uses the format of the police procedural, in which the protagonist is a professional police detective rather than a brilliant amateur in the Sherlock Holmes/ Nero Wolfe tradition. There is also, as with *Along Came a Spider,* a background of relationships between the police, their superiors, their partners, and other law-enforcement agencies. Patterson again shows Cross in his private life and describes the price he pays to be in his profession: long hours, low pay, and constant guilt at the time he is taking away from his family, especially his two small children, who have no mother (she died before the series began in an as-yet unsolved drive-by shooting).

Patterson also repeats the romance motif he introduced in *Along Came a Spider,* although in this case, the outcome is left open; Cross's relationship with a woman named Christine may well turn out to be long-term, unlike the terminated relationship in the earlier novel. Setting is another similarity between the two novels, with *Along Came a Spider*'s gothic element repeated in *Cat & Mouse*'s use of dark, labyrinthine train tunnels that create a sense of terror that may come from any direction and at any moment. Patterson's use of horror is, however, intensified in this novel by the descriptions of exceedingly graphic murders of victims who are kept alive as long as possible while they are being sliced to death.

An important genre element in *Cat & Mouse* comes from the classic mystery and detective formula. In the second of this novel's plots, the focus is on the search for an unknown murderer who turns out to be the least likely suspect, a device perfected by such Golden Age mystery writers as Agatha Christie (1890–1976) and Dorothy Sayers (1893–1957). Finally, Patterson once again uses elements of the sociological novel in his references to the callous disregard of crime in the inner cities, even by the police who are charged with containing it. At one point in the novel Alex Cross comments that racist cops in D.C. have a nickname for the worst ghetto areas: "They call them 'self-cleaning ovens.' You just close the door and let it clean itself. Let it burn" (162).

PLOT DEVELOPMENT

One of Patterson's favorite devices is the use of a prologue to begin his novels (he does this in each of the novels considered here), and in the case of *Cat & Mouse,* with its two separate plots, he begins with two prologues, one focusing on Gary Soneji, the killer first introduced in *Along Came a Spider,* and the second on a serial killer known only as "Mr. Smith." Soneji is in Washington, D.C., on a scouting visit; having escaped from prison in the earlier novel, he is now planning the murder of Cross and his family. Mr. Smith, meanwhile, is in London and is in the act of slowly murdering Drew Cabot, a Chief Inspector with Scotland Yard. After this brief introduction the story line returns to Soneji, who is setting up a spree killing in D.C.'s Union Station as a birthday treat for himself. He has taken as his role model the real-life killer Charles Whitman, who in 1966 climbed a tower at the University of Texas at Austin and shot students at random in a similar spree killing set in a public place. Such association of actual crimes with the fictional crimes that Patterson invents for Soneji adds plausibility to the story as a whole; readers know that similar events have taken place and therefore they accept them in fiction, too, even though they seem to be motiveless crimes.

As Soneji begins selecting and shooting his victims, Cross and his partner John Sampson are sent into the station with a cadre of police, but Soneji escapes. He goes to his home in Wilmington, kills his wife and ties up his daughter, then goes on to New York's Pennsylvania Station, where he stabs three more strangers. At the same time, the Smith killings continue in London, although the primary focus remains on Soneji and Cross, who has now been sent to New York to pursue Soneji (because of his earlier work on the Soneji case described in *Along Came A Spider*, Cross is considered an expert on his behavior and likely actions). Cross discovers as part of his investigation that Soneji has contracted AIDS while in prison and that he is now dying, and thus he has nothing to lose by this rash of new killings. Ultimately Cross corners Soneji in the tunnels of Grand Central Station, where Soneji kills himself, caught in the explosion of his own bomb. This would seem to be the end of the Soneji storyline in the novel, but instead, Cross and his family are attacked in their home in what appears to be a fulfillment of Soneji's threat that he would come back from the dead and avenge himself on Cross. This creates a new puzzle; who has attacked Cross's family, and why? The attacker turns out to be Simon Conklin, Soneji's childhood friend, who is carrying out Soneji's last wish. He does not succeed in actually killing Cross or his family though, only in hurting them badly.

The plot then switches to a second protagonist, Thomas Pierce, a brilliant FBI operative who specializes in tracking serial killers such as Smith. Cross, who is brought into the case by the FBI because of his background in psychology and his experience with Soneji, deduces that Pierce is actually Smith and thus Pierce begins as a protagonist and then becomes an antagonist. When Pierce is identified as the second killer, he tries to kill himself in the same way that he has killed his victims, performing a living autopsy on his own body. Ultimately he is shot by Sampson, sparing the reader a particularly gruesome death scene. The novel then ends with Cross proposing to Christine Johnson, a woman he has become involved with during the course of the story.

CHARACTER DEVELOPMENT

Alex Cross is the central character and the protagonist or hero of *Cat & Mouse,* just as he was of *Along Came a Spider.* He is a well-rounded character, although in this novel, he is static; he ends the novel as the fine policeman, father, and friend he began it and while he has clearly developed from the first novel to this fourth novel, the development has happened between books rather than as a part of this plot. When *Cat & Mouse* opens, Cross's wife Maria has been dead for six years and he has finally come to terms with this death. His goal is to "have some kind of normal life now. Not just a career, not a series of murder investigations" (51), although any canny reader knows full well that a normal life for Cross will indeed involve a series of murder investigations since his role as detective is the rationale for the Cross books. Much of the background on Cross has been filled in for the reader in *Along Came a Spider,* with additional details given here that build on rather than repeat this information. Thus, he still lives with Nana Mama, the grandmother who brought him up when his parents were killed, and he still has the same best friend and partner, John Sampson, although there is a bit more information in *Cat & Mouse* on how that relationship began when Cross and Sampson reminisce about meeting one another. In that first encounter the nine-year-old Sampson taunted Cross, who then retaliated. Sampson says, "I couldn't believe you would tangle with me. Nobody else would do that, still don't. Even back then you didn't know your limitations" (231). Thus, Patterson makes the point that Cross has always been brave and has always stood up for himself—admirable traits in a hero.

There are a few more details here about Cross's family background; he comments on the fact that his older brother was a junkie "before he died," an ominous statement which is left to stand as it is (the brother remains nameless, and whether or not he died as a result of drugs is open to the reader's imagination, as is any relationship he may have had with Cross). Cross remains the good-looking man he was in *Along Came a Spider*—the six intervening years have been kind to him and he is described here as "handsome as sin" (14). His lover Christine says of him, "*You're* the beautiful one. You are, you know. Everybody says so" (184). Finally, while Cross's two children have grown since the first novel, they still have the same warm, loving relationship with him as in previous books.

There are, however, more details on Cross the professional in *Cat & Mouse* than in the previous novels, particularly on the reputation he has gained within his field. He is repeatedly singled out by reporters at individual crime scenes, and when he is in New York, assisting with the case of the death of a New York policeman, he notes, "I enjoyed . . . the anonymity I felt in New York. In Washington, many reporters know who I am. If I'm at a homicide scene, it's usually a particularly nasty one, a big case, a violent crime" (153). It is this recognizability, this touch of fame, that brings him to Gary Soneji's attention in both *Spider* and here again, in *Cat & Mouse;* Soneji craves fame, and what better way to achieve it than by being associated with a famous investigator. Here, Patterson is using a standard technique of the classic mystery, where the detective's stature is measured by the cases he or she takes on. Sherlock Holmes is a great detective because he solves great crimes; he is a master detective who can defeat master criminals, and readers would be sorely disappointed to find that Holmes devoted himself to investigating, say, the cases of lost pets. Following this analogy, when Cross devotes himself to the capture of Soneji, Soneji, in his own mind, gains in stature; he is so good that he deserves the very best, and in Cross, he has it.

Another significant protagonist is Cross's long-term partner, John Sampson. However, Sampson exists only in terms of his relationship to Cross; his is a flat character in that there is no information on his background, his education, his reason for joining the police force, his dreams and aspirations. He is also a static character, ending the novel as he begins it. With the exception of one scene, Sampson's function in the novel is to help fill out the picture of Cross. At six foot nine, dressed in black leather, and wearing Wayfarer sunglasses, Sampson pairs with the six-foot-three Cross to create a sense of power; when they walk down the street, the weight of the law and of imposing physical force is in their bearing. Patterson plays off this heroic image by having Sampson be so sure of his masculinity that he can undercut it. Cross says of him, "Sampson liked to talk as if we were girlfriends in a Terry McMillan novel . . . which is unusual for men, especially two tough guys like us " (89), and it is because of their very toughness that they can afford to relate in this way—no one could mistake them as anything but sources of masculine power. However, this scene tells the reader more about Cross than about Sampson, since there are many other characters that Cross relates to, giving the reader a context for his interchanges with Sampson. In contrast, there is no information on Sampson's relationships with other characters and therefore no comparable contexts for his relationship with Cross. He is here to add to Cross as a character, rather than being a fully developed character in his own right.

The third significant protagonist is Christine Johnson, the woman with whom Cross falls in love in *Cat & Mouse.* A tall, beautiful woman, she is the principal of the school that Cross's two children attend and, like Cross, she also lost her spouse to a meaningless murder when he was shot in her presence in their home. Unlike Cross, though, she has had only six months to accept the death, and she is far less certain than he is about the possibility of building a new relationship, particularly one with someone like Cross, for whom violence is a constant fact of his professional life. In this way, she adds to the police procedural aspects of the novel by showing how hard the profession is on those involved with the police, and she also demonstrates the healing process that has taken place for Cross in the interval between the end of *Along Came a Spider* and the beginning of *Cat & Mouse.* Here, Cross is certain that he is ready for a commitment and it is Christine who is hesitant. There is little other information given about Christine and at the end, when Cross proposes to her, the reader is left wondering what her answer will be, leaving it speculative as to whether or not she has changed over the course of the story.

Cross's children, Damon and Jannie, are the children everyone would like to have; they are good-looking, intelligent, loving, and well-behaved, serving as a testament to Cross's parenting skills. They are here only in relationship to Cross—whatever life they may have with friends outside the home is left to the reader to guess—and as with Sampson, they are here to fill out the picture drawn of Cross rather than to be individuals in their own right. Like Christine Johnson they do, however, add to the conventions of the police procedural with their frequent comments about how much they miss their father, whose regular absences are a natural corollary of his profession.

The final member—and in many ways the most significant member—of Cross's family is Nana Mama, the grandmother who brought him up after the death of his parents. She is a superb mother figure, a woman who is always available to Cross and his children, and Cross tells the reader that she was just like that when he was growing up, too (83). She is a very intelligent woman, a retired school teacher who taught English, history, and Boolean algebra, and who serves as Alex Cross's conscience throughout this series. Her background information is somewhat limited from novel to novel, since the reader lacks details on her childhood and on how she came to be the well-educated woman that she is. She is, though, one of the few developing characters in *Cat & Mouse* since in this novel she is aware of the fact that she is growing older, knowledge that comes to her when she is playing Mozart's Concerto no. 21 and then has "a memory of how I used to be able to play it, a long time ago" (132).

In addition, there are a number of minor protagonists in the roles of the other policemen who move in and out of both the Soneji and Mr. Smith cases. Of these, the most interesting is New York Detective Manning Goldman, the oldest Manhattan homicide detective still working the streets, a man notorious for his rudeness to his colleagues. Cross's first impression of Goldman is that he is arrogant, but as he watches him work he decides Goldman is actually pretty good, which is high praise from Cross. Goldman's scenes are so brief that the reader learns little about him, and the fact that he is killed off early in the novel means that he has no opportunity to develop. Nonetheless, he remains an intriguing character, one that the reader would like to learn more about.

Cat & Mouse has two major antagonists, Gary Soneji, the psychopathic kidnapper/killer introduced in *Along Came a Spider,* and Mr. Smith, the torturer/killer introduced in this novel. Of the two, readers have the most information on Soneji, even those who have missed *Along Came a Spider* and have read only *Cat & Mouse.* He fits the usual profile of the psychopathic killer, beginning his career by killing neighborhood pets when he was a child, graduating to the murders of his family, and ending with fantasies of himself as a famous kidnapper and spree killer modeled on such notorious criminals as Bruno Hauptmann, the kidnapper of the Lindberg baby, and Charles Manson, killer of film star Sharon Tate. His given name is Gary Murphy, and he has adopted the name Soneji (pronounced *son-ee-gee*) because he thinks it sounds scary. It is also possible that he has adopted it because it was the name of one of his teachers, someone whom he alleges abused him when he was a child, or again it could be that he looks on his criminal self as the child of his natural self, and thus he is the "Son of G" or "Son of Gary." In this interpretation Gary Murphy has created a monster, the son of himself. Soneji is obsessed with Alex Cross because, like him, Cross is also famous. As noted before, it as though Soneji can acquire fame from Cross, from being investigated by him; only a master criminal deserves the attention of a master detective such as Cross. In his description of Soneji, Cross says he is "single-minded, obsessive, but he was also completely whacked-out" (106). He is very intelligent, another characteristic that makes him a worthy antagonist for Cross, and in *Cat & Mouse* he is drawn as a developing character, since he is slowly becoming less and less in control of his actions, a characteristic probably attributable to the fact that he now has a fatal disease and being careful gives him only a short-term benefit—as the novel begins his killing days are close to over, and will not out-last the story itself.

A second, minor antagonist is Soneji's childhood friend, Simon Conklin, who has attacked Cross's family as a final favor to the dead Soneji before being killed himself. Although the reader is given very little information on Conklin, he is given the novel's most memorable physical description: "He was tall and gangly and painfully thin. His milky brown eyes were distant, as if he were someplace else. He was instantly unlikable" (343).

A final major character falls into the classification of both protagonist and antagonist. When he is introduced as Thomas Pierce, he is one of Patterson's most attractive heroes, a cross between John Sampson and Alex Cross. Like Sampson he is tall, nearly always wears sunglasses, and with his long blond hair worn in a ponytail, he is the ultimate in cool. Although he is a member of the FBI's Behavioral Science Unit (the unit responsible for investigating psychopathic killers), he is, another law officer comments, "nothing like any agent [she'd] ever met or worked with" (119). He is known to be a hot-shot profiler (that is, excellent at drawing up psychological profiles of unknown perpetrators based on the crimes they have committed), and just as Cross holds a doctorate in psychology, Pierce holds one in medicine, backgrounds that give each special expertise in their hunting of killers. He and Cross also share the burden of loss; each has lost the person dearest to them—Cross through the murder of his wife and Pierce through the murder of his lover. Pierce has been assigned, at his own request, to the Mr. Smith investigation, even though Smith is responsible for the murder of his lover. Having Pierce on the case is a testament to his virtually irreplaceable skill, since it is most unusual to assign an investigator to a case in which he or she is directly involved with a victim.

Pierce's unusual background, his great intelligence and skill as an investigator, and the fact that both Sampson and Cross respect him and work well with him prepare the reader for a hero in the making, and it comes as a complete shock when Pierce is revealed as the torturer killer, Mr. Smith. Cross is as stunned as the reader. He says that Pierce "Doesn't fit any of the psychopathic profiles. . . . He's an original" (383). In fact Smith, with his loving, middle-class family, is "normal," or as normal as any of us gets, and one of the book's most chilling moments is when he tells the reader, "I'm human. I'm perfectly normal. I'm just like you" (391). Smith has killed his lover because he has discovered that she is having an affair. Does this mean that any of us might do the same? Well, experience seems to say that we might well do so (most murder victims are killed by someone close to them—a husband, a wife, a boyfriend, and so on), but it is highly unlikely that after this initial death we would then go on to become serial killers—there is a great difference between killing one's lover in the heat of passion and killing strangers at random.

In terms of categorizing Pierce/Smith as a round or full character, his very idiosyncrasy makes it difficult to do so. He doesn't fit the usual spree-killer pattern, and there is no hard information on what, if anything, in his background led him to become such a killer. This would make him a flat character, one with few dimensions. However, he is so interesting, in part because of his similarity to Cross, that readers find themselves filling in details for which there really is no evidence; we want to know more about him and so we create information to fill that need. As to whether or not he is a developing character, this is also a difficult determination to make; surely he ends the novel as violently disturbed as he began it and so the only evidence of change is that, like Soneji, he becomes less organized and less careful, characteristics that lead to his discovery. Since this can be seen as part of a continuum of deteriorating behavior that is apparent from the beginning, it is best seen as a continuation rather than a new aspect of character.

SETTING

James Patterson is an author who focuses primarily on plot, and for this reason, setting plays a minor role in his novels, serving to create a mood rather than to provide a motivating force for the action. This is the case in *Cat & Mouse,* whose most memorable description of place is that of a crack house in Washington, D.C., where "ten or twelve men and a couple of women were sitting or sprawled on the floor and on a few soiled, incredibly thin mattresses. The pipeheads were mostly staring into space, doing nothing. . . . It was as if they were slowly fading . . . into the smoke and dust" (167). Cross's ability to blend seamlessly into this environment works well to show that he is an authentic child of Washington's crime-ridden Southeast and that despite his educational and professional successes, he is still close to his roots.

The other significant use of setting in *Cat* is that of Union, Penn, and Grand Central railroad stations. Patterson connects them with Gary Soneji's childhood cellar experiences, showing how these dark, interweaving underground spaces have come to represent safe havens for him. With these exceptions, though, this is a novel that rests on plot rather than place.

POINT OF VIEW

Patterson makes an interesting use of point of view in *Cat & Mouse,* one that he will repeat in *Roses Are Red.* His usual pattern is to use the first person point of view (the "I" voice) for his major protagonist and third person omniscient, in which an unknown outsider who is aware of everything that is happening tells the story, for the sections that are told from the perspectives of all other characters. In *Cat & Mouse,* though, two separate characters are given first person narrations, Alex Cross and Thomas Pierce. This has the effect of associating them as dual heroes in readers' minds, which is exactly what Patterson intends, since Pierce first appears in the guise of a protagonist, an FBI investigator who is definitely a good guy in the search for Mr. Smith. Thus, the reader identifies both with Alex Cross and with Thomas Pierce through the use of the "I" voice for each of these characters. This is a technical device that allows readers to feel what Cross and Pierce are feeling, to think what they are thinking, to puzzle over what they puzzle over. In this way it allows readers to become investigators along with the novel's professional detectives, so that as they make discoveries the reader also does. In *Cat & Mouse* this use is particularly deceptive. Because Pierce is presented from the same perspective as Cross, the reader accepts him as an equally trustworthy narrator, and it is therefore shocking when he turns out to be one of the two serial killers—the detective is not, after all, supposed to be the criminal, and in Pierce, Patterson is making use of the "least likely person" motif, first introduced by the writers of the 1920–1939 Golden Age of mystery writing. These classic authors specialized in having characters seemingly above reproach, such as the family butler, the town doctor, or the vicar of the local church, be revealed as the murderers, people as unlikely in these roles as Pierce is in his. Mystery aficionados often play a reader's game with themselves in which they look at the full cast of characters, decide which is most unlikely to be the criminal, and then read on to see if this person is indeed the villain. It would be interesting to see how many of them would choose Pierce for this role.

Once Pierce is revealed as Mr. Smith, point of view again shifts. All events from Mr. Smith's perspective are narrated in third person omniscient, as though only legitimate heroes are worthy of first person narration; they are the only characters the reader is meant to identify with.

THEMATIC ISSUES

The unpredictability of human behavior is a major theme of *Cat & Mouse.* In real life it is impossible to predict how different people will react to the same events, and this worldview is carried through in *Cat & Mouse.* An excellent example of this is Gary Soneji. Abused and mistreated as a child, he has become an adult who abuses and mistreats others, behavior that is certainly common in real life and that any reader would be justified in predicting as his future. In the same way, Thomas Pierce, whose lover has betrayed him, murders his lover in retaliation and then becomes a serial killer, each time acting out the original murder, and this too might be predicted on the basis of human behavior. On the other hand, Alex Cross was orphaned as a child, along with his two brothers. The children were separated and brought up by different relatives, an experience that resulted in one brother's becoming a drug addict and the other dying of cirrhosis of the liver brought on by alcohol abuse, again, outcomes that could be predicted, given their growing up in Washington's crime-ridden African American ghetto. Cross, however, became someone who works to eliminate those who make drugs available to people like his brother, to make life in the ghetto better, and to provide desperately needed social resources for those whose days must be spent there. The reader thinks, "How come? What was there in Cross's life that was absent from his brothers'?" And Pierce, who constantly re-lives the murder of his beloved, is doomed to a life of destruction whereas Cross, who has also experienced the murder of his beloved, goes on to heal himself and help others in the process. This is almost the opposite of what one would predict for the two characters. Cross has had the disrupted childhood, whereas Pierce has had, by all accounts, a stable, loving childhood. It is Pierce who would seem the best candidate for self-healing, for going on to make a fulfilling life for himself once he learns of his lover's betrayal. Instead, it is Cross who becomes a good father in the face of a dysfunctional childhood and a good citizen in the face of a life lived in the midst of crime that kills both his brother and his wife. It would seem then that Patterson's theme here is that life is unpredictable. At best, we can guess what people are likely to do, and our predictions are likely to be flawed.

ALTERNATIVE READING: A RHETORICAL ANALYSIS

One way of studying literature is by examining parallel structures within a work or even outside of the work, as when one novel is compared to another (an excellent example of parallel novels is Lawrence Durrell's *Alexandria Quartet,* in which three separate novels examine the same events from different points of view). Lee T. Lemon (*Approaches to Literature* 1969) notes that such parallelism can be based on units of any size—clauses, sentences, paragraphs, chapters, and so on–and he says that this technique "of suggesting thematic values by creating parallel structures designed to be compared and contrasted is one of the most pervasive of all literary techniques" (169). He expands on this by noting that when parallelism is applied to characters, "one of its major purposes is to suggest some of the considerations necessary for the realization of the theme of the work" (170). Such parallelism is a particularly useful way of analyzing *Cat & Mouse* because its two major characters, Alex Cross and Thomas Pierce, mirror one another in significant ways, while their differences lead to an understanding of theme.

When Cross and Pierce are introduced, it appears that they have much in common and little to contrast them. Physically, each is a tall, handsome man and neither fits the expected description of a policeman. Cross holds a doctorate in psychology from Johns Hopkins, and Pierce holds a medical doctorate from the equally prestigious Harvard—hardly typical backgrounds for law enforcement officers. Both are well known in their respective fields, Cross with the Washington police and Pierce with the FBI Behavioral Science Unit, so much so that whenever the press learns that either man is assigned as an investigator to a case, they automatically assume that the case will consist of a bizarre crime or crimes. Cross and Pierce even share the same nickname—both are called "Doc" by the journalists writing about their respective cases. The two men are relatively close in age—Pierce is 33 and Cross about 44 in this novel—and both are experts at profiling, the art of projecting the personality and behavior patterns of psychopathic killers. It is also significant that both work well with John Sampson, Cross's partner, who begins by assuming that Pierce is an effete, intellectual Harvard boy and comes to respect him as a hardworking investigator and a man as capable of strenuous physical work as is Sampson himself.

A significant similarity between Pierce and Cross is that each has lost someone he loved dearly. In Pierce's case, four years before the events of *Cat & Mouse,* his long-time lover, Isabella Calais, has been murdered in what is assumed to be the random crime of a psychopath; similarly, six years before the story begins, Cross's wife Maria is also murdered, the victim of a drive-by shooting. For each protagonist this meaningless loss is the central climactic event in his life, one that becomes the motivating force for subsequent actions.

Clearly, there are many striking similarities here: How many professional investigators are doctors? How many have graduated from prestigious universities? How many have become widely known to the public at large? And how many have lost the central character in their lives to a random killing? However, when the contrasts between the two characters are examined, the reader learns that Pierce plays a double role: he is both protagonist and antagonist, and it is he who is responsible for having murdered his lover as retribution for her having an affair. This raises the question of why Patterson has patterned his antagonist so closely on his protagonist. The most obvious technical advantage to his doing so is deception—the reader simply does not expect a protagonist to turn out to be the antagonist, especially not when he is patterned on the novel's hero. However, in addition to deception this device also has an effect on the stature of the novel's actual protagonist, Alex Cross.

First of all, the technique of parallelism in *Cat & Mouse* adds credibility to Cross, since it reinforces the concept that a man as well educated as he might indeed choose to become a professional investigator—if Harvard graduates make such choices, so too can Johns Hopkins graduates. The technique also lends plausibility to Cross's becoming something of a press celebrity, since the same thing has happened to Pierce—what is true of one policeman can easily be true of another.

More importantly, though, the pairing of Cross and Pierce in this way reinforces the importance of Cross's response to his wife's death and ultimately adds to his stature as a human being. Cross has been terribly hurt by a random act of violence, and his response is to devote his life to eliminating violence from the lives of others. He does this not only through his job but also through his activities in the community, where he provides free psychiatric counseling to the homeless. In contrast, Pierce, a medical doctor who has also been permanently scarred by violence, never uses his skill to heal but only to hurt—his method of killing is to essentially perform autopsies on his living victims. In each instance, a gifted, highly educated man has suffered a traumatic event, but in one case it has motivated the man to become a person who works to cure others, while in the second case it has motivated the man to become a person who works to destroy others. Pierce says that each time he kills someone in his role as Mr. Smith, he is acting out the original murder of his lover—here, violence begets violence; by extension, each time Cross helps someone, he is acting out his redemptive response to the murder of his wife, and so for him, violence begets goodness.

In this way, the technique of parallelism between protagonist and antagonist creates a philosophical statement about human beings and how they act in the world, highlighting the choices open to us for good and for evil. It is significant that Pierce, who chooses evil, ends up killing himself, and Cross, who chooses good, ends up proposing marriage to a new woman who has entered his life. Although the reader does not know if she will accept the proposal, what matters here is that Cross has made it, that he is ready now to put the tragedy of his wife's death behind him and go on to make a new life. Thus, one man destroys any possibility of healing while the other creates such a possibility, a contrast that is highlighted by Patterson's technical device of pairing his major characters in *Cat & Mouse* and that leads to the theme that while human beings are helpless to control random events, they can indeed control their reactions to them.

8

Pop! Goes the Weasel (1999)

In *Pop! Goes the Weasel,* James Patterson has become very comfortable with his stable of repertory characters: Washington, D.C., homicide detective Alex Cross, his children Jannie and Damon, his grandmother Nana Mama, and his partner and life-long friend, John Sampson. The novel is based on the assumption that readers have become thoroughly familiar with Cross through earlier works, and for this reason, only the barest information is given on this group—if we've been following Cross we already know them, and so we need only a few reminders as to who they are and how they relate to one another.

Patterson makes use of a structure in *Pop! Goes the Weasel* that is similar to his earlier Cross novels; once again the story begins with a prologue that introduces the major antagonist, and once again this antagonist is a serial killer. The novel then switches to the main action of the story, with each chapter designed almost as a sound bite; at two to five pages in length, the chapters are quick to read, mimicking the effect of watching a television show. In a *Seattle Times* interview, Diane Wright quotes Patterson's long-time editor, Michael Pietsch of Little, Brown, who says of this effect that Patterson's "pages turn really fast, and there's a velocity to the reading that's part of the pleasure. He wants to boil down the chapters so that, whether it's a point of drama, a point of character or a point of emotion, he hits that point clearly and hard, and moves on" (2003, E4). The novel as a whole takes the form of the "how dunnit," in which the reader knows who the killer is and the mystery then becomes, "How will he be caught?" rather than, "Who did it?" Here, Patterson repeats a form he first used in *Along Came a Spider*. This time, though, the answer is straightforward; the person identified in the prologue as the "who" does indeed turn out to be the villain, without the sleight-of-hand switching of villains that Patterson has used in other novels such as *Kiss the Girls*. In those stories the reader says, "Ah, it's him! Oops, no, it's her! Hmm, it must be someone else." In contrast, in *Pop! Goes the Weasel*, the villain turns out to be the person he was alleged to be at the very beginning.

Another favorite Patterson technique used again in *Pop! Goes the Weasel* is that of multiple plot lines. There are four main ones here, the first centering on killings of prostitutes in Southeast Washington, D.C., the second on the antagonistic relationship between Cross and his supervisor, the third on Cross's ongoing romance with Christine Johnson, and the final plot on an elaborate role-playing game that includes the serial killer as one of its participants. Finally, Patterson also utilizes here the open ending first seen in *Kiss the Girls*, an ending that leaves the reader with an antagonist who is still on the loose and who could, and more than likely will, strike again, a very good technique for an ongoing series in which the author thriftily keeps all options open for subsequent stories.

GENRE

Once again, Patterson is working in the police procedural genre in which the emphasis is on the day-to-day routine of the working policeman (see Chapter 2 for a more complete discussion of this genre). There is the usual emphasis on the difficulties of the job itself, and on how hard it is on family life. Patterson also develops the concept of the bonding of partners who must work with and depend on one another in life-threatening situations, a realistic element of the police procedural since it so closely mimics the actual working life of policemen. And, just as in reality most crimes are solved by routine procedures, in *Pop! Goes the Weasel* significant clues are run down through such mundane means as checking motor vehicle records. There is also realistic discussion of why some crimes are more difficult to solve than others as when Cross tells the reader, "Prostitutes make for difficult police investigations. . . . On average, a hooker . . . might turn a dozen or more tricks a night, and that's a lot of forensic evidence just on her body" (120).

An element of the procedural that Patterson carries over here from *Jack & Jill* is the frequent antagonism between the working detectives and their superiors. These superiors are often seen as far more concerned with good public relations for the department, and hence the preservation of their own jobs, than with the solving of crimes, a concern that leads them to focus on high-profile crimes at the expense of those involving the poor and powerless. Chief Pittman, Cross's superior, carries this even further than is usual in the police procedural since he personalizes his hostility toward Cross; he is convinced that Cross is after his job and is out to discredit him, which seems a bit odd since Cross has good results in his cases, brings credit to the department, and shows no evidence of aspiring to any other position (in fact, if he were, it would probably be to a private practice in psychology). Pittman has enlisted another detective, Patsy Hampton, to spy on Cross and report everything he does in the hope of undermining him professionally and eliminating him as a competitor. In the traditional police procedural the police support one another, even in the face of a hostile bureaucracy, and it is unusual that Hampton would take on such an assignment, although she does eventually alert Cross to the machinations of Pittman.

Finally, there is much of the sociological novel in *Pop! Goes the Weasel*, wherein there is stinging comment on the greater society as it impacts the events of the story and the lives of the characters. Thus, as the novel opens, Cross is taking some boys to visit their fathers in prison and he says, "The thing about most of the prisoners . . . was that they knew what they had done was wrong; they just didn't know how to stop doing it" (15). This is the compassionate remark of someone who understands the circumstances that lead to crime. Cross volunteers at a soup kitchen in his neighborhood and he tells the reader, "I watched the usual lineup of men, women, and children who had no money for food. . . . It seemed such a pity, so unfair that that so many folks still go hungry in Washington . . . (33). It is a typical observation of Cross's that Washington, D.C., the capital of the United States and the place that should be our national jewel, is home to such poverty and squalor and has become a setting where "the neighborhood youth activity is the crack trade" (41).

Cross lives in Southeast, a predominantly African American section of Washington, and when a crime is committed there, its investigation is cursory; there's no money for assigning extra detectives to the Southeast, although corresponding unsolved crimes in the powerful establishment enclaves of Georgetown and the Capitol district would, we are told, enrage people. One of Cross's African American colleagues says that if such a high level of open crimes were the case in those neighborhoods, "Be *Washington Post* headlines every day. The president himself be involved. Money no object. National tragedy!" (56). This setting plays an important part in the murders, since the killer chooses it deliberately, saying that he's killing people in the poorer sections of D.C. because "nobody cared about them anyway" (106). It is noteworthy that this comment is accepted as factual—it's just the way things are here. A friend of one of the victims says to Cross, "The police won't do nothin'. You never come back here again after today. You don't care about us. We're nothin' to nobody" (126), and Cross does not disagree with her. As a reaction to the official response to crime in Southeast, Cross and four of his close friends form an unofficial group of detectives who investigate specific crimes in the area on their own time, when they're off-duty, and while Patterson leaves this particular plot strand undeveloped in *Pop! Goes the Weasel,* it has clearly caught his imagination since he comes back to it and expands on it in a somewhat different guise in his later novels *1st to Die* (2001) and *2nd Chance* (2002).

PLOT DEVELOPMENT

Pop! Goes the Weasel opens by introducing Geoffrey Shafer, an ex-agent with MI6 (the British equivalent of the CIA), who is now with the British embassy in D.C. He has become a serial killer and is suicidal. He has, with three other ex-agents, created an elaborate role-playing game in which his role is Death. The three other players are Conqueror, Famine, and War, and it would appear that all have committed murders as part of the game, although this is left open to the reader's imagination—it may be that only Death plays out the game in reality, that for the other three it is just an elaborate fantasy. The relationship among the four is reminiscent of that between Casonova and The Gentlemen Caller in *Kiss the Girls,* who give support and validity to one another in their pattern killings.

Death has a secret existence in which he is a gypsy cab driver, and picking up fares is the method he uses for isolating victims. He goes through a complex dice-throwing ritual to determine how each fare will be treated: some go unscathed, others are tortured and violated. This is how he meets Nina Charles, an African American nurse at St. Anthony's hospital in Southeast who is a beloved figure in her neighborhood. The dice go against her and she is killed in what Alex Cross has come to call the Jane Doe murders. By his count, there are well over a hundred of these, most involving prostitutes or drug addicts, but his superiors in the D.C. police refuse to accept his view of these deaths; they prefer to see each as a random killing with no relationship to any other. Cross is initially assigned to the Charles case but is then removed to work on the case of a German tourist robbed and killed in Georgetown, a very upscale area of D.C. This is only one instance in which the reader is reminded that in D.C., some deaths are more important than others.

When Cross and his four friends band together to investigate the Charles case on their own time, their Chief of Police suspends three of them and sets a fifth detective, Patsy Hampton, to spy on Cross and report to him. Hampton quickly comes to the conclusion that the Jane Doe murders are indeed related and that Geoffrey Shafer, a.k.a. Death, is the perpetrator. She tells Cross what Pittman is up to, begins following Shafer, and is murdered by him. At this point the focus of the novel shifts to Shafer and his multiple killings, as well as to the group of role players, and the plot strand of Pittman out to destroy Cross is abandoned, at least for this story, although there is acceptance of the fact that the Jane Doe murders are indeed connected, completing the second plot.

A strong tertiary plot is that of Cross's romance with Christine Johnson. Each has lost a spouse, and each is a handsome, successful African American choosing to work in D.C.'s Southeast (Johnson is principal of an elementary school there). *Kiss the Girls* ends with Cross proposing to Johnson, and the reader is left hanging—there is no response. In *Pop! Goes the Weasel* Cross proposes once again, and this time, Johnson accepts. It would seem that a routine happy ending is in store, at least as far as this particular plot thread goes, but then Johnson is kidnapped by Shafer and his companions in the fantasy game. The reason for the kidnapping is only hinted at; Shafer wants to include Cross and his partner John Sampson in the game, and this is apparently his way of doing so, although why he wants them in the game and what role they are to play is never made clear. At the end of the novel Johnson is rescued, now the mother of a baby named Alex, a child that she conceived with Cross just before the kidnapping occurred. How the relationship will now develop is again left unanswered, leaving readers open to a continuing storyline in a subsequent novel or novels.

In the meantime, Shafer is arrested for the murder of Patsy Hampton and waves his diplomatic immunity in order to clear his name. A courtroom scene follows, and Shafer is ultimately found innocent. However, the British Security Service has taken an interest in Shafer, the game, and its players, and is convinced that Shafer is indeed guilty. Meanwhile, the three other players drop out of the game, deciding that it is just too dangerous to continue with this group fantasy/reality. All the players come together in Jamaica, ostensibly to discuss the situation, although Shafer believes that their real purpose is to kill him and eliminate the greatest source of danger to them. Before they can do so he kills them, ending the plot strand of the game and how it will develop. Shafer is then supposedly killed by Cross in an underground water battle. However, this being a James Patterson novel in which answers constantly turn into questions, Shafer manages to escape Cross, return to London, murder his wife and then disappear so that, once again, the reader is left with an open ending, one that may be resolved in a subsequent work, a type of ending that is often found in series works, in which the author may well want to keep his or her options open where particularly strong characters are concerned.

CHARACTER DEVELOPMENT

If the information in *Pop! Goes the Weasel* were the only information readers had on Alex Cross, Patterson's protagonist or hero, he would seem a flat character; there is very little here on his childhood, education, family background, and so on. However, this is because Patterson is assuming, and in most cases rightfully so, that readers have already gathered this information in earlier Cross novels, where it is spelled out in detail. *Pop! Goes the Weasel* confirms the character Patterson has previously established for Cross, with some few additions; he is still helping out in the soup kitchen at St. Anthony's church, a church in his neighborhood, he is still working as a liaison between the D.C. police and the FBI in the Violent Criminals Apprehension Program, and he is still considered to be an outstanding profiler of psychopathic killers. At 41 years old he is a handsome man, and still reminds people of the young Muhammad Ali. Family, consisting primarily of his children and Nana Mama, the grandmother who brought him after up after his parents' death, continues to be a central element of his life and he remains the good father he has been drawn as in the previous Cross novels.

The only change in *Pop! Goes the Weasel* consists of Cross's acceptance of the senseless murder of his wife Maria in an unsolved drive-by shooting some six years ago. Where in earlier novels he is still grieving for her and attempting to come to terms with her death, in *Pop! Goes the Weasel* he has accepted the fact that his wife's murder may never be solved, and he has transformed the pain of that into his motivation for continuing to work as a homicide detective: "Maybe that's what drives me to solve every case I can, no matter how bad the odds" (34).

While Cross is, for these reasons, relatively flat in this novel (that is, a character about whom we are given limited information), he is a dynamic or changing character in that besides accepting his wife's murder, in his professional life he has become a loner who ignores the orders of his superior and continues on with his private investigation of the Jane Doe murders, an action that suggests he has gained in self-confidence and that his reputation has grown to the point where he can afford to do this—it is difficult to be a loner in a bureaucracy and only exceptional people succeed in that role.

The second major protagonist of *Pop! Goes the Weasel* is Cross's long-time partner, John Sampson. Here, too, the character is sketched rather than developed in detail, as though Patterson knows that his readers are already familiar with Sampson and thus only need to be reminded of key details, such as the fact that Sampson and Cross have been friends since they were nine years old, that Nana Mama is a mother figure for both of them, and that each has total faith in the abilities and commitment of the other. Sampson does have a girlfriend, Millie, in this novel, although her name is all we learn about her. Possibly this is a strand that Patterson will develop in future Cross novels.

Pop! Goes the Weasel also has a group of intriguing protagonists who are carryovers from *Jack & Jill* and *Cat & Mouse:* Jerome Thurman, Rakeem Powell, and Shawn Moore. All are homicide detectives from the First District with connections to Southeast, and along with Sampson, they have been meeting with Cross to work on the Jane Doe killings in their own time since, as noted above, these killings are being ignored by the police establishment. This activity results in everyone but Moore being suspended from the force. Cross's suspicion is that Moore was kept on as a divide-and-conquer technique on the part of their supervisor, so that the other detectives will distrust Moore and feel that he had betrayed them; if so, it is a technique that does not work, since the members of the group remain loyal to one another. The fact that these men risk their jobs to work with Cross on this case says much about Cross's appeal as a leader, and perhaps helps to explain his supervisor's paranoia about him. At novel's end all three detectives are reinstated, and while their roles have been small, most readers will hope to see more of them in subsequent works, since they add texture and credibility to the police procedural aspects of the Cross series by filling in the background of Cross's daily routine as a detective.

Nana Mama, the grandmother who raised Cross after his parents' death, remains the staunch, intelligent, caustic, and loving center of the

Cross family. As always she serves as Cross's conscience (or at least he says she does), and as always, she is an advocate for the need for more opportunities and respect for African Americans. Although her role in *Pop! Goes the Weasel* is minor, Patterson gives her one delightful scene, a flashback in which, at the age of about 54, she decides that the boys Cross and Sampson must learn to swim, and enrolls both them and herself too in Red Cross lessons. Her reason for this: "The majority of people in Southeast didn't know how to swim back then, and she felt it was symbolic of the limiting inner-city experience" (184).

In terms of antagonists or villains, Patterson again has created a psychopathic killer who murders for the sake of murdering rather than because of any personal involvement with the victim. A very handsome 44-year-old man (Patterson seems to have only handsome protagonists and antagonists), Geoffrey Shafer is the most well-rounded of the four antagonists who appear in *Pop! Goes the Weasel* because we know the most about him; he was trained as a spy for Great Britain's MI6, he has a beautiful wife and three children, all of whom he loathes, and a job with the British Embassy in D.C. that he equally loathes. The job is, in fact, a way of sidelining him, since he is no longer considered an effective agent and yet his wife's father is a powerful enough figure that it would be politically difficult to let Shafer go. He is heavily dependent on pharmaceutical drugs including Thorazine, Librium, Benadryl, Xanax, and Vicodin, which he obtains from a psychiatrist he is having an affair with, and he has become suicidal in his risk-taking. At various times Patterson describes him as hyper, manic, and bi-polar. As a child, Shafer describes himself as a bully, someone with "a natural mean streak, a vengeful, nasty way" (203). His father was an abusive military man and his mother, often beaten by the father, died in a fall when Shafer was 12. He has two older brothers, both highly successful businessmen, and he says that it was in MI6 that he found his true calling and learned that not only could he kill another human being, he actually enjoyed doing so.

With the end of the Cold War there is no longer a professional role for Shafer and he now lives for what he calls "the game," a computer fantasy based on the Four Horsemen of the Apocalypse, allegorical figures in the Book of Revelation in the Bible. Shafer's version of the game is played by four players who all have connections to MI6. They have been playing it for seven years, making it more involved and complicated as they go along. There is Oliver Highsmith in the role of Conqueror, the rider on the white horse; James Whitehead in the role of War, the rider on the red horse; George Bayer in the role of Famine, the rider on the black horse; and Geoffrey Shafer in the role of Death, the rider on the pale horse.

Such a game with such characters lends itself to an allegorical interpretation of the novel. A classic allegory is a story that works on more than one level, so that besides the literal meaning of the story itself, it has a second meaning in which characters, events, and setting represent ideas and concepts beyond themselves. The most famous allegory in English literature is John Bunyan's *Pilgrim's Progress* (1678), which traces the journey of a protagonist, Christian, who achieves salvation by fleeing the City of Destruction and journeying with much travail to the Celestial City. However, in *Pop! Goes the Weasel,* the allegory is undeveloped since the four players are seeking simply the novelty of an unusual fantasy or adventure and it is more than likely that only Shafer plays out the fantasy in real life. He does this by creating a second persona for himself in D.C., in which he disguises himself as an African American and drives a gypsy cab, that is, a taxi that is privately owned rather than one that is part of a professional fleet. This allows him to go anywhere in D.C. and appear to be legitimate, just another taxi driver with a fare. The game is governed by throws of the dice with various combinations dictating various plays, although these combinations are never clear to the reader—only enough information is given to suggest how seriously Shafer takes the fantasy. In the role of Death Shafer has committed the Jane Doe killings and, as the novel unfolds, he becomes more and more out of control, until he no longer abides by the rules of even the fantasy game, going against the rolls of the dice. In this way he is a dynamic character, or a character who changes from the beginning of a story to its end, since he is now a character who can no longer control his actions. When he kills the other players in the game, fulfilling his role of Death, he escapes, goes on to kill his wife, and disappears until such time as Patterson may choose to reintroduce him in another novel.

The remaining antagonists are the other players in the game, flat, static characters since we know almost nothing about them except their particular roles (we don't even know why they have the specific roles they each play) and they remain the same throughout the novel, characters whose significance resonates through Geoffrey Shafer's need of the fantasy they all play rather than through any actions of their own.

SETTING

The major setting of *Pop! Goes the Weasel* is the artificial or man-made Southeast section of Washington, D.C., a very poor, crime-ridden, predominately African American area of the capital. It is a place where water stands in stagnant pools around blocked drains, where whites are a curiosity, and where graffiti tells the departing visitor, "You Are Now Leaving the War Zone and You Lived to Tell About It" (14). Setting is integral to the novel in that it determines the killer's choice of victims; he chooses people from the poorest sections of D.C., and because these poorest sections are the African American streets, Southeast becomes his hunting ground. Setting also determines his use of disguise; to blend in, he must appear to be African American and this in turn deflects attention from him, since the few sightings of the killer report him as an African American male (something Cross finds surprising; he says that the highest percentage of serial or pattern killers are Caucasian, and of course the reader trusts his information; he is a specialist in this particularly gruesome area of crime). Another imaginative use of setting is the cab that the killer drives. Rusted and taped up, it fits right in as a poor man's gypsy cab, reassuring would-be riders at the same time that it helps to camouflage Shafer.

Natural setting is virtually nonexistent in *Pop! Goes the Weasel.* There are a few references to the beaches of Bermuda and the high, hidden villages of Jamaica, but for the most part, these settings could be anywhere and contribute little to the motivation of characters or the actions of the plot.

POINT OF VIEW

As is customary with his Alex Cross novels, Patterson once again uses a split point of view in *Pop! Goes the Weasel,* with all the scenes focusing on Cross being told by him in first person, or "I" point of view, and those focusing on other characters being told in third person omniscient, in which an unidentified narrator who knows everything becomes the narrative voice. The "I" voice works well for Cross in that it allows the reader to identify with him and essentially to become Cross, pursuing the investigation with him, sharing his love of Christine and his children, his great fondness and exasperation with Nana Mama, and the bond he shares with John Sampson, while the third person narration gives the reader insight into matters closed to Cross, such as Chief of Detective Pittman's use of departmental spies against him. In this novel, the use of the third person also has the effect of isolating Cross, so that he is seen as embattled; if he cannot trust the people in his own department, he is indeed an outsider, a lone hero in the classic American tradition of such iconic figures as *Shane* (1953).

THEMATIC ISSUES

The most prominent theme in *Pop! Goes the Weasel* is that we live in a world of betrayals. Examples of this happen over and over again throughout the novel. Superiors betray inferiors, colleagues betray colleagues, spouses betray spouses, doctors betray patients, teammates betray teammates, and even nature betrays human expectations of it. Chief of Detectives Pittman betrays Alex Cross by using a fellow detective to spy on him, hoping to find evidence that will allow him to fire, remove, or transfer him. The fellow detective is also betrayed, since to set a colleague against a colleague is to create a world of secrecy and intrigue in which one colleague is striving to incriminate another. Patsy Hampton, the detective Pittman uses against Cross, in turn betrays Pittman by alerting Cross to Pittman's plans. While this may seem like the noble thing to do since Hampton is convinced that Cross is an exemplary detective, she does it in an underhanded way; that is, she could have gone to Pittman and said something on the order of, "Look, this assignment is baseless. Cross is a fine policeman and I really can't continue with this." Instead, she pretends to Pittman that her surveillance of Cross continues at the same time that she alerts Cross to Pittman's schemes. Here, Hampton is protecting her job rather than her ethics. Hampton is in the vulnerable position she is in because early in her career she made a serious procedural error and this was reported by another detective, "a jealous older male" (98), an act that has allowed Pittman to have leverage over her actions. Once again, then, a colleague has betrayed a colleague, and once again it is for personal rather than professional reasons.

In terms of partners betraying partners, Geoffrey Shafer is having an affair outside of his marriage, and in a very weird way his serial killings can also be seen as betrayals of his wife, since there is much sexual content and gratification for him in the acts. Shafer is in turn betrayed on a number of fronts, first of all by the psychiatrist he sees who provides him with drugs and who is having an affair with him. This is a profoundly serious breach of the patient/doctor relationship, as well as an equally serious breach of ethics on the part of the therapist. He is also betrayed by his fellow game players, who are apparently conspiring with one another to kill him. This is being done not because Shafer is thoroughly out of control, which he obviously is, but because the remaining three players want to protect themselves. Shafer anticipates these actions and kills the players before they can kill him; in other words, he betrays them before they can betray him.

Finally, in *Pop! Goes the Weasel,* even nature betrays. Alex Cross and Christine Johnson go to Bermuda to escape the violence of D.C. and enjoy the promised tropical paradise of endless white beaches, blue waters, peace, and quiet: a place as close as human beings can get to Eden on earth. Instead of the anticipated paradise, Christine is kidnapped and taken to a desolate, isolated, very poor area, which is ironically also located in the tropics. In short, then, this is a novel in which nothing can be taken at its face value and betrayal constantly threatens.

ALTERNATIVE READING: THE GENERIC NOVEL

Chapter 2 has much detail on the various genres of popular fiction, and notes that James Patterson's work crosses genres, making use of the conventions of many different types, of which the most dominant is the police procedural, a dominance that increases with the continuing development of his series thrillers, the Cross novels and the number novels (*1st to Die* and *2nd Chance*). Because the police procedural falls into the broader category of mystery and detective fiction, much can be learned about Patterson as a mystery and detective author by analyzing the extent to which his work does and does not conform to the conventions of this broader genre.

In the classic mystery, stories are composed with an easily identifiable beginning, middle, and end. In the beginning, a crime is committed, usually murder, and if not murder, then a crime significant enough to be worthy of the efforts of the detective—a theft on a grand scale, a kidnapping that threatens death, and so on. Patterson consistently works a variation on this beginning, in which he starts his novels with a prologue, usually one that identifies the killer (although often by a pseudonym the killer has created) and shows the type of crime that this killer commits. It is only after this that the novel switches to the conventional opening, in which the serious crime is committed, and at this point the reader usually knows who the criminal is, although the true identity may be hidden by the pseudonym used. The question to be answered in the mystery now becomes how will this identity be uncovered and how will the criminal be stopped, rather than the more traditional question of "Who Done It?"

The middle of the conventional detective novel is announced by the entrance of the detective, and now the reader follows the detective as he or she finds clues and recognizes patterns that will lead to the solution. Here, Patterson is absolutely true to the model; this is exactly what Alex Cross does in his investigations.

At the end of the traditional mystery, the reader is given the solution, the detective explains how he or she reached this solution, and the murderer is disposed of (usually through arrest or suicide). Patterson uses all of these conventional endings and adds yet another; in both *Kiss the Girls* and *Pop! Goes the Weasel,* a killer goes free. This allows Patterson to reintroduce a strong villain in a later novel and, at the same time, build on reader-identification with particular characters, a most economical device for any writer of a series.

In addition to a neat beginning, middle, and end, there also tends to be a standard sequence of events in the classic mystery. First of all, there is a stable society at rest. This is not necessarily a good, moral or just society; it is simply a known society, operating on its usual day-to-day patterns. In the Cross novels, this society is Southeast Washington, D.C., a very poor African American neighborhood made up of the gamut of inner city inhabitants, from Cross's wonderful Nana Mama, a brilliant and ethical woman with a despairing worldview based on her life in Southeast, to the homeless people Cross helps to feed at Southeast's St. Anthony's church, to the doomed inhabitants who live in crack houses, seeking their own destruction and that of everyone around them, to the people who believe that the world really can be a better place, a place of integrity and achievement, such as Christine Johnson, the principal of Sojourner Truth School and Cross's lover.

The next step in the usual sequence is the commission of a serious crime, one that disrupts the day-to-day life of the community. While it would not seem possible that disruption caused by crime could come about in routinely crime-ridden Southeast, some crimes are so out of the ordinary that they do indeed disrupt the predictable and expected; this is true of the Jane Doe murders since, in this area, murder usually happens for some identifiable reason such as drugs, money, or passion, not out of the blue and for no apparent cause, as they do here.

In the classic model the commission of the crime is typically followed by the introduction of the detective, whose task it is to discover who committed the crime. In *Pop! Goes the Weasel* Patterson uses an interesting twist on this convention. His detective, a Washington, D.C., policeman, takes on this task not as part of his regular working life but as an extra charge, since there is little interest among the D.C. police establishment in solving crimes in areas like Southeast, where crime is seen as a sort of self-correcting mechanism ordained by nature wherein undesirables are removed by other undesirables, a process that should be allowed to take its natural course. This adds an extra element of suspense to the story;

now it is a story not only about whether or not the detective can figure out who is responsible for the crime, it is also about whether or not he will be allowed to do so.

At this point the focus of the classic mystery shifts to the tracking down of clues and gathering of pertinent information, after which the inquiry is completed and the solution announced, steps that Patterson faithfully adheres to. The criminal in such a mystery is then disposed of, and it is here that Patterson again deviates from the usual generic pattern. His killer escapes and goes free, presumably to continue on with his pattern of serial killings. Where the traditional mystery and detective novel would now end with a restoration of society to its state before the commission of the crime, Patterson does not give the reader this solace; of course Southeast remains its crime-ridden self. However, the serial killer also remains on the loose and could conceivably return to Southeast or a similar neighborhood at any time. In other words, this specific evil has not been eliminated from society.

There are also conventions that apply to the detective, and here Patterson conforms to the generic pattern whereby the detective is the focus of attention, something Cross certainly is in *Pop! Goes the Weasel.* And although there are scenes here in which the criminal is the focus, these are always overshadowed by Cross and his actions, in large part because of the use of first person in all the Cross sections, causing the reader to identify with the detective—we are in his mind, and for this reason, his activities become ours.

The classic detective must also be able to recognize and connect clues, something Cross does in a highly organized manner, writing notes on index cards which he then posts on the wall of his attic office, seeking and finding patterns that lead him to a solution. Once he reaches a solution, he has successfully completed the detective's basic task, that of finding the criminal.

In terms of the character of the detective, there are also conventions that apply. Typically the detective is a romantic hero who represents the possibilities of the individual: he is smarter than the average person, braver, and able to overcome barriers that many find insurmountable. This is shown in the case of Cross by his superior education and his rise to a position of authority with the D.C. police department despite the poverty of his childhood in a D.C. ghetto; not many people growing up here earn doctorates from Johns Hopkins University or successfully face down a Director of Detectives. The romantic hero is also defined by his or her strong code of ethics, although they are likely to be situational ethics, in which the moral values of an action depend on the situation rather than on a black-and-white code of right and wrong. An excellent example of this is Cross continuing with the investigation of the Jane Doe murders even though he has been ordered to desist. Here, Cross follows his instinct that this should be done rather than honoring the orders of his superior, something that ethically he is also required to do. As Patterson has created the narrative, the reader sides with Cross in this dilemma; of course he should continue to work on the Jane Doe crime. The ethical imperative to do so is clearly greater than his obligation to his superior.

The detective in this genre is also noteworthy in that he crosses all social boundaries (which Cross does despite the fact that his being an African American would seem to shut him out of many social settings), and he gets to know people well, probing into their lives, their pasts, and their sins in ways that, in reality, it would be most unlikely a stranger could do. The fact that Cross is a psychologist is of great help to him here and adds strongly to his credibility as the romantic detective, the person who can know all, since certain professions lend themselves to such disclosure on the part of strangers: journalism, the legal profession, the ministry, and Cross's own profession of psychology are all excellent examples of this.

As to the general characteristics of the genre, the world of mystery and detective fiction is a world in which there is always an answer. In real life, we are often left with unsolved crimes, and the fascination of these is apparent in the number of books that are written seeking to pose solutions to such actual mysteries as who killed Lizzie Borden's parents, who really kidnapped the Lindbergh baby, what happened to Jimmy Hoffa, and more recently, who killed Jon Benet Ramsey. It is as though human beings have a craving for closure, and this is a craving that is met in the fictional mystery; here, instead of life's unsolved crimes, we always know who did it, who was at cause. This makes the genre an optimistic one; even though it often features much blood, gore, and violence, overall it tells the reader that answers and solutions can be found by people who know where and how to look, by people dedicated to the search for truth. The underlying philosophical stance is that the universe is logical and that justice is possible, a stance supported in all of the Alex Cross novels.

Thus, for the most part Patterson adheres to the pattern of the mystery and detective genre, with some variations in the beginnings of his novels and the disposition of his criminals. Overall, this means that any reader of Patterson's works will leave them with a sense of closure; the world is indeed knowable, as the example of Alex Cross shows us.

9

Roses Are Red (2000); *Violets Are Blue* (2001)

The novels *Roses Are Red* and *Violets Are Blue* are linked novels, with the second work completing the major plot line begun in the first. Of the two, *Roses Are Red* is the richer novel, setting the groundwork for what will follow in its sequel. This groundwork is intricate, involving three different plot strands, only two of which are resolved in *Roses Are Red*. The third is resolved in *Violets Are Blue*, and, while *Violets* also has more than one plot strand (a technique that is typical of Patterson's work), the strongest part of this novel is its completion of the previous work.

GENRE

Roses Are Red is a police procedural, "the subgenre of mystery and detective fiction in which the mystery is solved by the police as part of their professional duties" rather than being solved by a brilliant private detective such as Sherlock Holmes (Kotker 2001, 617). All of Patterson's Cross novels share, to some extent, the use of this genre. However, *Roses Are Red* is the purest example of a procedural in the Cross series, with its focus on the actual work of the police, the methods by which crimes are solved, and the cost to individual policemen of the demands of the job. When, early in the novel, Cross is investigating a bank robbery, he begins by searching out his street contacts, small-time criminals who will give information to the police that is typically based on gossip they have access to as part of the criminal world. Cross says that he has "a couple of tattered black notebooks filled with names of street contacts" (22–23), and although he and his partner have already talked to some two dozen of them, they could easily spend the next three days covering the rest. Later, he emphasizes that this is the way police work actually goes: "You put out a lot of nets, you checked them, and every so often something was actually in one of the nets. More often than not, it came from a relative or friend of the perp" (250).

There is also authentic information on the way various agencies interact with each other, particularly the FBI with local police forces. When the FBI is called in, the FBI takes over, and it has become almost a cliché of police work that the federal agents are condescending and patronizing to the locals. And while in real life it is unlikely that Alex Cross, a detective with the Washington, D.C. police, would be working in case after case with the FBI, Patterson has created a plausible reason for this; Cross, as a psychologist, is a specialist in profiling serial killers and acts as the FBI's Violent Criminal Apprehension Program's liaison with the metropolitan police.

Another aspect of real-life police work is that, unlike private detectives, most notably the amateur detectives of fiction, very few policemen have the luxury of working on only one case at a time. Usually, there are a number of investigations going on at once, from stolen cars to home break-ins, drug trafficking, domestic violence, theft, and homicide. If one were to take a snapshot of the average work week of a police detective, at the end of the week some cases would be solved and others would remain open, still being worked on. This pattern has become a convention of the fictional police procedural in which, typically, the most important cases are solved and minor ones are left hanging, a convention Patterson uses at the end of *Roses Are Red,* where there is resolution to only two of his three plot strands and readers must go on to *Violets Are Blue* for the answers to the third. A final convention of the procedural that Patterson emphasizes in *Roses Are Red* is the disruption the job causes to normal family life. There are a number of instances here where Cross cannot be with his children at important times because he is away on a case, and this is a constant source of tension between Cross, his children, and the grandmother who acts as mother to them.

As he has done in the earlier Cross novels, in these two works Patterson makes use of the romance genre with its basic theme of "true love triumphant against all odds" (Rosenberg and Herald 1991, 143), and as he has before, he inverts the pattern here so that for Alex Cross, once again true love turns out to be defeated, with Cross's beloved former fiancée breaking off the relationship, seemingly for good. This failed relationship also fits into the pattern of the police procedural; it is directly attributable to the strains and dangers of Cross's life as a homicide detective since the fiancée, who has nothing to do with the police or F.B.I., has been victimized by criminals because of her relationship with Cross.

PLOT DEVELOPMENT

Roses Are Red has three simultaneous plots: a bank robbery and murder case that is the central crime being investigated by Cross, the illness of his daughter Jannie, and the relationship between Cross and Christine Johnson. The novel opens with a prologue that constitutes chapter one and describes the original situation, in which bank robberies are being committed at the direction of someone called the Mastermind. A series of complications now begins with the F.B.I.'s Kyle Craig (an ongoing character from earlier Cross novels) calling in Cross for assistance because something is quite out of the ordinary in these robberies—families are taken hostage and killed even though they cooperate fully, bank employees are killed without reason, and the bank robbers themselves are murdered in grotesque ways. Cross says, "It almost seemed that a serial killer was robbing banks" (76), since, as one of the F.B.I. agents notes, "Bank robbers don't usually kill anybody. Not pros" (53).

There is a total of five robberies, of which the fifth is the most dramatic, involving the hijacking of a tour bus whose passengers are taken as hostages. A 30 million dollar ransom is demanded and paid in a clever drop done from a train that has the police and F.B.I. so exhausted from following the conflicting commands they receive over a number of hours that it is plausible that this heist would actually succeed. In the climax, the kidnappers are caught not by clever police work but instead by being informed on by the daughter of one of them, who is seeking revenge for her father's brutal treatment of her mother. This too is a highly credible ending, following, as noted in the section on Genre, the pattern of how most crimes are solved in the real world; someone tells.

The kidnappers lead to the Mastermind, who then turns out not to be the Mastermind after all but, instead, a patient of his. And in true Patterson tradition, this new Mastermind is also not the real one. On the very last page of the novel, the reader learns that Kyle Craig, the F.B.I. agent who is working with Cross on this case, is the actual Mastermind. However, Cross does not yet know this—he leaves the novel still searching for him, and so for Cross and the police agencies working on the robberies, the case is still open—it is only readers who are privy to Craig's identity as Mastermind. Because of this, *Roses Are Red* lacks a denouement, or a final wrapping up, of its major plot thread, which has been left to be resolved in its sequel, one that is most appropriately titled *Violets Are Blue.*

The second plot strand centers on Cross's beloved 8-year-old daughter Jannie. In this plot's original situation, Jannie is a pretty, witty, playful child, very bright and an eager participant in family activities, including learning how to box along with her 10-year-old brother. Complications begin when Jannie has a seizure after being hit in a boxing lesson. She has a second seizure and then a third, and in the climax to this subplot, she is diagnosed with a brain tumor. In the denouement the tumor is successfully removed and Jannie returns to her usual life and even to her boxing lessons with her brother, having been assured that the seizures and being hit were unrelated. Her illness highlights Cross's guilt about being unable to be with his children as much as he feels he should. It serves to show that Cross is a loving parent, and that his role as a parent is complicated by his job—the work that he does is important and being a parent is important, too, and policemen, more than most professionals, often have to choose between their responsibilities at home and their responsibilities at work.

The effect of the profession on one's home life is also at the heart of the third plot strand. In this strand's original situation, Cross's fiancée, Christine Johnson, has returned to Washington, D.C., after having been kidnapped and held hostage for nearly a year, a scheme planned by a serial killer whom Cross investigated in an earlier novel. During the captivity Johnson gave birth to Cross's child, Alex, Jr., and Cross's family and friends are now having a party to celebrate the baby's christening. However, Johnson has been traumatized by the kidnapping and lives in terror that the serial killer, who has been identified but has not yet been caught, is coming back for her and that her association with Cross puts her in mortal danger. This story line climaxes in Johnson's decision to leave Cross and the D.C. area. In the denouement the baby stays with Cross, adding another member to this family of delightful children, loving grandmother, and single parent.

CHARACTER DEVELOPMENT

As with all the Alex Cross novels, Cross himself is the main character and protagonist. He is sketched in rather perfunctorily in *Roses Are Red* as if by this, his sixth appearance as hero of a James Patterson novel, his creator can assume that readers already have a good deal of information on him and need only be reminded of certain key aspects that have contributed to his development. The first of these aspects is his childhood. Cross was orphaned when young and was then brought up by his grandmother, known throughout the series as Nana Mama. She is a voice of wisdom and of love, and Cross considers her to be his conscience. Cross is also defined by his role as a father; he is loving to and well-loved by his children, Damon and Jannie, and throughout the series has hopes of finding a mother for them to replace his wife Maria, who was killed in a drive-by shooting.

Another aspect of Cross's character is his loyalty as a friend. Throughout the series his relationship with John Sampson is emphasized, from their childhood friendship to their adult roles as partners on the Washington, D.C., police force. Cross's relationship with F.B.I. agent Kyle Craig is also indicative of his commitment to friendship. They have been friends for years, they have worked on many different serial-killer cases together, and Cross has great respect for Craig's abilities. This respect and friendship may well contribute to Cross's inability to see that Craig is himself a serial killer, that he is the Mastermind.

A dominant thread of Cross's character that is particularly noted in *Roses Are Red* is the attractions that his job holds for him. Why, after all, should a man who has a Ph.D. in psychology spend his time working as a homicide detective, with the severe disruptions that this causes to his family life? He searches for answers to this and questions his motivations, wondering if it is the danger and fear that are inevitable parts of the job that are the causative agents, if it is "The adrenaline spike that wasn't like anything else I'd ever experienced? The uncertainty of each new case? The thrill of the hunt? A dark side of myself? . . . Good occasionally triumphing over evil? Evil often triumphing over good?" (78). The robberies and kidnapping under investigation here are a case, he says, that "Both fascinated and repulsed me" (108), and when an agent asks him if he likes being a homicide detective better than being a psychologist, he answers, "I do. I love the action" (290). It is clear that he is very good at this job he loves, since the F.B.I. asks him to assist on key cases.

In this novel, Cross is also something of a fatalist. He accepts that Christine cannot live with him, that her fear simply will not allow her to do so, and that there is nothing he can do to change this. He is a good boxer, he has self-esteem (he will not allow a large, heavy, violent mental inmate to intimidate him by calling him "nigger") and at age 41 he is still a handsome man who looks very much like the prizefighter Muhammad Ali "at his best" (81). His stress release, playing jazz and classical piano, remains the same here as in the earlier novels. These characteristics combine to make him a rather flat character in *Roses Are Red*. However, for fans of the series he will remain a round character since he has been developed in the preceding Alex Cross books and readers will use their background knowledge to fill out the Cross they meet here. As to whether Cross is best described as a static (unchanging) or dynamic (changing) character, in *Roses Are Red* he best fits the definition of a static character. He ends the novel as he began it, a single father troubled by the demands of his job and yet loving many aspects of it, a devoted friend and a lonely man who is hoping for a meaningful relationship with a woman who can be not only his companion but also a companion to his motherless children.

Of the remaining protagonists, three are characters carried over from earlier novels, Cross's partner, John Sampson, his grandmother, Nana Mama, and his one-time lover, Christine Johnson. All appear here as minor figures and have little opportunity to develop, given that they are onstage for such a short time. Nonetheless, the information provided is consistent with what readers have learned about them in earlier books. Sampson and Cross grew up together in poverty-stricken Southeast Washington; they bonded early and have remained loyal friends ever since. They must make very impressive figures when they confront criminals, with Cross at six foot three and Sampson at six nine. Between them, they surely create the impression of superheroes out to defeat evil. As to Nana Mama, she has raised Cross since he was nine years old and she is, Cross says, the best psychologist in the house. Cross thinks of her as his conscience and it is she who impresses on him that his children are an obligation just as his job is, that they too need his attention. Readers wanting to know more about her, particularly about her perceptive and scathing comments on the workings of power in America, will need to consult earlier Cross novels.

The final protagonist, Christine Johnson, also plays a minor role, her main function in the novel being to act as a graphic illustration of how difficult it is to be a part of a policeman's life. She cannot recover from the terrifying experience of having been kidnapped and held hostage because of her association with Cross. She tells him, "I *can't sleep* nights. I have nightmares all the time. I can't concentrate during the day. I imagine terrible things happening to little Alex. To Damon and Jannie and Nana, and to you. I can't make it stop!" (91). The fact that Cross, a psychologist, cannot help her demonstrates the depth of her fear and makes plausible her leaving Washington, and her leaving her child behind strongly suggests that the final cost of her having become involved with a policeman is that she can no longer cope with any level of responsibility. Since the reader is given little background on Christine other than her kidnapping, and since she ends the novel in the same state of terror in which she began it, she is both a flat and a static character.

A character who is difficult to place as a protagonist or antagonist, since he plays both roles in the novel, is the F.B.I. agent Kyle Craig. He and Cross have worked on a number of serial killer cases and it is he who is responsible for bringing Cross into the investigation of the robberies and kidnapping. In his role as protagonist, he is drawn as a highly competent agent, one for whom Cross has much regard. However, this description is a light sketch only, since the reader knows little about his background, about what attracted him to the job, about his goals, his loves, and his hates. He would have to be characterized as a developing character since he turns out to be the villain rather than one of the novel's heroes, but only the reader knows this. For Cross, Craig remains the same at the end as he was at the beginning.

In his role as antagonist, Craig is more fully developed. The reader learns that he is compulsive in his attention to time and detail, that his planning is meticulous, that, like all Cross villains, he exults in feeling superior, in being a master criminal, and that he prides himself on perfection. His crimes are based on his need for revenge and his hatred of the establishment, although the reasons for these strong, violent feelings are left ambiguous. He is aware that he is not normal, saying of himself as he rapes a woman he has just killed, "I'm a ghoul. . . . I'm crazy . . . and that's the biggest joke of all. *I'm the one who's crazy.* If the police only knew. What a great clue" (139). As is clear from the tone of his thoughts here, he takes joy in his otherness, and he shares with Cross the love of danger, saying that this is what "got his adrenaline flowing and turned him on" (274). For the reader Craig is a developing character, since he goes from protagonist to antagonist. However, this is a revelation that will have to wait for *Violets Are Blue* before Cross, too, is privy to the change.

Finally, the novel has an intriguing set of sub-villains in the various groups of bank robbers and hijackers. While none of these is fully developed, the light sketches that give them a sense of separate identities are intriguing and leave the reader wanting to know more about them. Thus, one set of robbers, a group of hardened killers, has the frivolous names of Mr. Red, Mr. Blue, Mr. White, and Ms. Green, names so unsuited to their actions as to add to their fearsomeness by suggesting that they take death and the inflicting of it lightly, as though death were a child's game based on colors. Even more fearsome is the villain Tony Brophy, an ex-con who is six foot four and a muscle-bound 260 pounds. He's dressed in "black paramilitary pants, off-white shower thongs, no shirt" and his upper body is "covered with jailhouse tats and curled black hair" (112). He fits everyone's image of a really bad guy and he has indeed been interviewed by the Mastermind as a possible recruit for the robberies, but, he tells Cross, "Guess he didn't want me for his crew." When Cross asks why, Brophy says, "He wants *killers,* dude. I'm not a killer" (114). If someone like Brophy, who would send chills down anyone's spine, is not bad enough for the Mastermind, this makes a strong statement about his inherent evil. Brophy is also a fine example of Patterson's ability to sketch a memorable character with just a few strokes; Brophy takes up only three pages of an almost 400-page book, and yet he remains in the reader's mind as an effective symbol of violence.

SETTING

Patterson's most consistently effective use of man-made or artificial setting throughout the Alex Cross novels is his searing descriptions of Washington, D.C.'s, Southeast section, the poorest part of the city. This is a scary, ominous place where everything seems to be in a state of rot and decay. When Sampson and Cross approach the First Avenue projects, Cross describes them as "abandoned tenement buildings where junkies and homeless people lived, if you could call it living, in America's capital city" (37). The two detectives are searching the buildings, looking for the bank robbers, in a setting where rats scurry away from the beams of their flashlights and the stench is unbearable. This is an abandoned project and one might expect that projects still functioning would be better, but this is not the case; the East Capitol Dwellings housing project, where Cross and Sampson continue their search, is, says Cross, a "subsidized human warehouse" that "looks like a failed prison. Cold, white cinder-block fences surround bunker-like buildings. It's thoroughly depressing and not atypical of housing in much of Southeast" (207). Unlike the First Avenue projects, it doesn't have the excuse of having been officially abandoned—this is functioning housing in the capital of the United States. Place descriptions such as this make strong statements about how America chooses to treat its poor, sick, and minorities, and add credibility to Nana Mama's outrage over conditions of life in D.C. When she points out to Cross that D.C. has the dubious distinction of being considered, by the Children's Rights Council, the worst place in the nation to raise a child, Patterson's thoroughly depressing settings have gone a good way to make her case for her.

The way people are dressed is also an aspect of artificial setting; we can learn a good deal about people from the clothes they wear and the styles they choose. The description of Tony Brophy in his black paramilitary pants accentuated by his jailhouse tattoos, identifies him at once as someone to be very wary of. Similarly, the description of a drug hustler dressed in "crimson nylon shorts over blue nylon pants, Polo T-shirt, Tommy Hilfiger windbreaker, Oakley shades" (35) is vivid not only in its styles and labels (Polo, Hilfiger, Oakley) but in the very colors Patterson chooses: crimson and blue. How could such a figure not stand out in the misery of Southeast D.C., and how could this image of money and success not have great appeal to poverty-stricken children who face a future with little hope? Such use of dress serves to highlight the conditions under which many people live in D.C., where some of the most obvious routes out of the ghetto lead ultimately to jail.

The only significant use of a natural setting in the novel is the description of Christine Johnson's beautiful flower garden, one that she has planted behind her apartment. It is filled with roses of different kinds and Cross says that it reminds him of the Christine who existed before her kidnapping, suggesting that, through this garden, she is attempting to recreate the life she once had. However, it is a garden that she does not own—it is planted on the rented soil of her apartment house—and the fact that she ultimately leaves it is a statement that, at least in this case, the beauties of nature can do little to temper the horrors perpetrated by human beings.

POINT OF VIEW

Patterson typically uses two points of view in his Alex Cross novels, first person and third person omniscient, and he follows this pattern in *Roses Are Red,* with first person for each chapter centered on Cross and third person for each centered on other characters, with one exception; in Chapter 103 of *Roses Are Red,* the Mastermind speaks and thinks in first person, although the point of view used for him in every other chapter in which he is the key actor is third.

The use of the "I" voice or first person is a very effective technical device for the Alex Cross chapters; it causes the reader to identify with Cross throughout the investigation. When he is puzzled, the reader is puzzled, and when he is angry, the reader understands the source of his anger. Another advantage to the use of first person in the Cross novels, including *Roses Are Red,* is that the reader, in identifying with the "I" voice, becomes an investigator along with Cross. One of the delights of mystery and detective fiction for many readers is working out the solution to the crime in the same manner as the detective does. When Cross gathers evidence and that evidence is shared with the reader, the reader too can become a detective, seeking to find the solution by the same means as Cross.

The one chapter using first person point of view that does not focus on Cross is centered on the Mastermind, who is watching Cross and exulting in the fact that Cross doesn't know that he is being watched, that he has no sense of how vulnerable he is to the Mastermind. Paradoxically, this chapter has the effect of causing readers to continue to focus on Cross just as they do in the chapters centering on him, because the reader has been so led to identify with him that fear for him has an element of personal fear for the reader, too. If, as we read the novel, we are at times Alex Cross, then when he is threatened so, too, are we.

Patterson's use of third person omniscient for the non-Cross sections of the novel is straightforward; he uses this technique to allow the reader to see what the robbers are doing and what is happening on the hijacked bus, information that Cross would have no access to. In some of his novels (see especially *Along Came a Spider*) Patterson has used this point of view to mislead the reader, giving partial information in the guise of complete information. However, in *Roses Are Red,* third person omniscient is used without deception and the reader can trust that a given character's thoughts and motivations are presented as they actually are, without significant elisions. This in turn has the effect of adding credibility to the novel's final revelation, when we learn, from a third person narrator, that Kyle Craig is the Mastermind, while Cross, in his first person view of the crime, has yet to discover this.

In many ways, *Roses Are Red* depends on *Violets Are Blue* for its theme and even for its possible alternative readings, since it is, by itself, an incomplete novel, one that has not been brought to full closure at its end. James Patterson has used continuing characters in many of his Alex Cross novels (Gary Soneji, Geoffrey Shafer, Katherine McTiernan, Cross's supervisor, his F.B.I. contacts, and of course, his partner and his family). However, *Roses Are Red* is the first of his Cross novels in which the story itself is a continuing story, carrying over into *Violets Are Blue,* the novel that follows it. In this way it is similar to a serial, although the classic serial was published in monthly magazine installments. Charles Dickens (1812–1870) was and is the master of the serial novel, a form that has gone out of favor among today's writers, with only a few exceptions; Norman Mailer's *An American Dream* (1964) and Stephen King's *The Green Mile* (1996) are rare contemporary examples.

Serials can be distinguished from sequels in that the serial completes significant ongoing actions, whereas sequels tell a new story about characters who have appeared in an earlier work or works. (There are also prequels—novels that utilize the same characters in a story that takes place before the first published novel in a series. This technique sometimes allows a writer to create a work that couldn't have been written after the first novel if, for example, the characters in the first novel had been killed at the end. The prequel enables the writer to use these characters again by explaining how they originally came to be. Popular films such as the *Star Wars* series make use of this technique, since it allows their creators more room for enlarging on the characters and themes first presented to viewers.) Holman and Harmon note that an identifying characteristic of the serial story or novel is its ending, which will be "a moment of suspense or surprise" (1992, 438), teasing the reader to go on to the next work, and this is exactly how Patterson ends *Roses Are Red.* Its final chapter consists of Kyle Craig and Alex Cross at the scene of the murder of Betsey Cavalierre, an F.B.I. agent with whom Cross had begun a relationship. Craig is saying to Cross, "I'm so sorry about Betsey," and at the same time, the reader is alerted to the fact that he is the Mastermind. *Violets Are Blue* then opens with Cross at the very same site, and while Craig is not there in person he is on the telephone, talking to Cross as the Mastermind. The question posed is, when will Cross discover that Craig is the Mastermind? Ah, we must read the rest of the new novel to find out.

GENRE

As is true of *Roses Are Red, Violets Are Blue* is also a police procedural, focusing on the everyday working life of a police detective with the Washington, D.C., police force. It also has trace elements of the romance novel in its protagonist Alex Cross's loneliness and search for a companion. These are combined with an emphasis on the horror novel and in particular, the vampire novel. Cuddon notes that vampirism "has inspired numerous horror stories" and that these "flourish from China to Peru." One of the first vampire novels was John Polidori's *The Vampyre* (1818), which, says Cuddon, has "little about bloodsucking in it and is mostly concerned with sex; as are many vampire stories" (1991, 421–22). The best-known vampire story is Bram Stoker's *Dracula* (1897), although for contemporary readers Anne Rice's vampire novels, particularly her first one, *Interview with the Vampire* (1976), certainly run a close second. Patterson follows the typical generic convention of combining sexual attraction with the attraction of blood, and much of *Violets Are Blue* is devoted to a pair of antagonists who feed on sexually attractive humans as if they were prey.

PLOT DEVELOPMENT

As with many of the novels in the Alex Cross series, *Violets Are Blue* has more than one plot, a technique common to the police procedural where the usual pattern is that many cases are being investigated at the same time just as they would be in real life. As discussed in Chapter 3, plots can usually be divided into four parts: the original situation, the complications, the crisis or climax, and the denouement. In the first of the *Violets Are Blue* plots, the original situation is that Cross is still seeking the identity of the Mastermind, picking up where he left off in *Roses Are Red.* Complications arise when the Mastermind continues to harass Cross with phone calls that the police and FBI are unable to trace. At this point, Kyle Craig is brought in to investigate the murders in the second plot and he requests that Cross be assigned to work with him. This then becomes a major complication to the first plot, since Cross does not know that the Mastermind he is seeking is the man he is working with. He continues to receive threatening calls and eventually discovers, almost by chance, that the Mastermind is Craig when he sees him staking out the apartment of a colleague. In the denouement, or wrapping up of the plot, Craig is connected to earlier crimes and FBI suspicions are confirmed. While he is on the run Craig targets and kills two of Cross's friends, but ultimately, Cross out-thinks him and finally captures him.

The second plot is the vampire story. In this plot's original situation, two people are running in San Francisco's Golden Gate Park, something they often do. Complications occur when they are attacked and killed, the man by a tiger and the woman by two humans. Cross has worked with Kyle Craig on a somewhat similar case in D.C. and so, when the FBI are called in, Craig requests that Cross be added to the team. Meanwhile, complications continue as killing follows killing, with the victims being hung by their feet so that they literally bleed to death. The murders then move to Las Vegas, Charleston, Savannah, Charlotte, and New Orleans. The reader already knows who the primary killers are—two brothers, William and Michael Alexander—but is unsure of the role played by two magicians and a character known only as the Sire, any of whom may or may not be directing the killings. Complications multiply when the magicians themselves become victims. The brothers return to California where they kidnap Jamilla Hughes, a San Francisco police detective and Cross's romantic interest in this novel. Cross and the FBI free Hughes, Cross finds and kills the tiger, and the brothers are killed. In the climax, Peter Westin, an academic expert on vampires, is identified as the Sire, the person in charge of a cult of vampires that have committed such murders over the past eleven years. In the denouement, the traditional wrapping up of a novel where the consequence or consequences of the action that has occurred in the climax is presented, the Sire tells Cross, "You have no idea. You have no clue how someone like me thinks" (317), and the reader is left to puzzle over the reason for these vicious murders.

CHARACTER DEVELOPMENT

In this novel protagonists are sparse; besides Alex Cross, there are just two, John Sampson, Cross's partner, and Jamilla Hughes, a San Francisco homicide detective. Sampson appears only in telephone calls and Hughes's main function is to serve as a possible future love interest for Cross. Cross himself, the central protagonist of this series, is now 42 years old and still a very handsome man. He is the most well-rounded of any of the characters in the book, since we know about his relationship with his children (loving and somewhat guilt-ridden because of the time he must spend away from them), his record with women (not good—everyone he's involved with seems to end up dead or traumatized) and his need to be loved, an observation made by the Mastermind, who sees this as "an obvious flaw" (230).

There is little information here on Cross's background in D.C., his education, his relationship with his colleagues and superiors, and his family life. All of this has been established in earlier novels and perhaps Patterson can safely assume that anyone reading *Violets Are Blue* is familiar with the series as a whole and already has this information. What Patterson focuses on here is the attraction of policing for Cross and also his ambivalence toward it at this point in his career. Cross explains to a colleague with whom he is on stakeout that the first case he solved was a drug-related murder in his neighborhood, one that would have been written off as just a fact of life in Southeast had he not become involved. He did this on his own time and when he had identified the murderer and solved the case he was hooked: "I knew I was good at [detection], maybe because of all the psych training I'd had, and I liked making things right" (224). Patterson also gives a good deal of information on Cross's working techniques; he immerses himself in a given crime scene, and after the technicians have completed their jobs, he typically wanders around a site for several hours. He says, "It's a ritual for me, part of my own obsession. Maybe I feel I owe it to the dead" (123–24). His intuition is superb. He has learned to trust it, and it is this that saves Jamilla Hughes from the Mastermind. Cross has no factual information that she is threatened and yet he follows his instinct that she is in immediate danger and it is this that saves her life.

Cross has, however, possibly reached the point of burn out in *Violets Are Blue,* in great part because of the negative impact of the job on his relationship with his family, made worse by the fact that he is a single father and therefore the only parent his children have. He questions whether he should leave the police but still feels driven by the work. An F.B.I. colleague tells him that he seems tense, and Cross lists his current anxieties, focusing on how the sickest, most bizarre cases "have affected every aspect of my life. I'm afraid they're changing who I am" (85). Even his childhood friend and long-time partner, John Sampson, has suggested that it may be good for Cross to make changes. Cross considers going into the F.B.I., although that would be very similar to what he does now, or going back into psychology, either practicing or teaching, but at this point in the novel, close to its beginning, neither option holds much attraction for him. However, by the last page of the novel he has come to a decision, making of him a developing character or one who changes; he will resign from the D.C. police. This may indicate the end of the Alex Cross series of police procedurals or it may signal a new direction for Cross and Patterson—a closure that is left unresolved.

If the novel is noticeably lacking in protagonists or heroes, it compensates by being rich in antagonists or villains: there is Kyle Craig, who is the Mastermind, William and Michael Alexander, the tiger-handling vampires, and Peter Westin, the Sire who directs the actions of the Alexanders and, presumably, those of other vampires. Craig is the most well-rounded or developed of this group. He is an F.B.I. agent who has worked with Cross for many years on high-profile serial killings and it is Craig who is responsible for Cross becoming the liaison for the D.C. police with the F.B.I., a position that makes Cross's possible transfer to that agency plausible. In the series as a whole Craig is first presented as a protagonist and it is only in *Violets Are Blue* that Cross learns he is an antagonist, a serial killer. He is very intelligent and highly skilled—Cross calls him the best homicide detective he has ever worked with—and he sees himself as a hunter, both of victims and of criminals. His reason for seeking out Cross as a colleague seems to be that he has great admiration for Cross's skills and feels that when he misleads Cross he demonstrates, to himself if to no one else, how very, very good he is; he is superior to the best. Why he became a murderer is unclear, although he does tell Cross that he was severely beaten for years when he was a child by a demanding, ex-military father, a detail that fits with the background of many psychopaths. Nonetheless, his development into a killer is something of a puzzle in that its motivations are unclear; he is not acting for money, for ideology, or for fame and the reader is left to conclude that he kills for the sake of killing. When he is finally caught by Cross, his character remains consistent; he is a killer to the end.

Another unusual pair of antagonists are the brothers William and Michael Alexander, 20 and 17 years old, respectively. They are exceptionally handsome and have been brought up in a commune set at an isolated California ranch. Their parents were hippies and also animal handlers, which explains their ability to handle the tiger who accompanies them on many of their kills. The brothers think of themselves as "the special ones" (56) and call themselves vampires. They've been killing for five years, although how they actually became vampires is left unanswered, and certainly, many children grow up in communes without becoming killers, let alone vampires. When at the end of the story Cross kills them, they remain as they began, intriguing but unexplained.

The final antagonist is another vampire, Peter Westin, a professor at University of California, Santa Barbara, who has an international reputation as an expert on vampires and vampirism. He is also the Sire, a sort of head-vampire who gives orders to other members of the cult, including the Alexander brothers. (Westin maintains that a vampire subculture exists in nearly every major city in America, although Patterson leaves this statement unsupported. Cross believes that there are people who think of themselves as vampires but he sees them as role-players, even when the roles they are playing become violent.) When Cross arrests Westin, Westin tells him that it would be impossible for Cross to understand him and his acts, and the reader too is left with this lack of understanding, which makes of Westin a flat, essentially unknown character who is unchanging throughout the novel.

SETTING

All the major settings in *Violets Are Blue* are man-made or artificial, and all have a staged quality that adds to the bizarreness of the story. One of the most striking of these is the Church of the Vampire, which, the reader is told, actually is a church with "vast, high-ceilinged rooms filled with . . . old Victorian furniture, elaborate golden candelabras, human skulls and other bones, tapestries that portrayed stories of famous old blood seekers" (88). Most of the people who frequent this church are role-players who pretend to be vampires, but this is a dangerous pretense; William and Michael use the church as one of their hunting grounds.

Another site that blends fantasy and reality is the Tattoo, Fang and Claws Parlor that Cross visits in Fresno, where he learns that almost all the frequenters of vampire clubs throughout the country wear fangs, and where he turns down the offer to have a set custom made just for him. This shop setting opens with an ugly scene of an unattractive teenage girl being tattooed and wincing as the needle punctures her skin, making the point that many people do choose to have their blood drawn for purely aesthetic reasons. This in turn makes it more believable that another reason for drawing blood would be the actual drinking of it. Not all the sites used are strange and ugly, though. Patterson includes the lovely East Coast cities of Savannah and Charleston and the garden district of New Orleans, and here the effect is to sharply contrast their beauty with the ugliness of what happens in the vampire culture there. Overall, in *Violets Are Blue,* setting serves to blur the line between fantasy and reality and so to add to the possibility that maybe there really are vampires such as William and Michael out there, prowling the United States—maybe it isn't all just make-believe.

POINT OF VIEW

As he did in *Roses Are Red,* Patterson uses two points of view in *Violets Are Blue,* with first person or "I" voice for chapters focusing on Cross and third person omniscient for chapters focusing on other characters. In both novels this has the same effect; the reader identifies with Cross but is an observer of others.

THEMATIC ISSUES

A central theme of both *Roses Are Red* and *Violets Are Blue* is the statement of the philosopher Schopenhauer that "Human existence must be a kind of error. It is bad today and every day it will get worse, until the worst of all happens" (74). When Cross quotes this, he says his own philosophy is a little cheerier, although he does not state exactly what his philosophy is, nor are we ever told what is meant by the "worst of all." Certainly there is much evidence here for Schopenhauer's pessimistic outlook. In *Roses Are Red,* Christine Johnson cannot recover her normal life and lives in terror, to the point where she leaves her child in order to establish a new life for herself. But in doing so she attains only the illusion of safety since, after she has done this, Cross must tell her to go to yet another place: the serial killer who traumatized her is still at large and has probably obtained her whereabouts inadvertently from Cross, who with this act shows that he cannot protect her. Added to this is the setting of Southeast Washington, D.C., where the fabric of urban life is either decayed or on the verge of decay and none of the powers that be seem in the least alarmed by this. Perhaps the "worst of all" that happens in this novel is that the major crime under investigation is not solved—the Mastermind goes free to kill again, his identity still unknown.

Violets Are Blue repeats this theme, first with Cross accepting the end of his relationship with Johnson and more importantly, with the revelation that Kyle Craig, F.B.I. agent and long-time colleague of Cross, is a psychopathic killer. The vampires who go from playing out fantasy roles to actually killing people are another instance of behavior deteriorating into "the worst," as is Cross's decision to resign from the D.C. police force at the end of the novel. It would seem that he has given up, that he has no hope of achieving justice through being a policeman and that in the face of this, the cost to him and his family is simply not worth it. At this point in the ongoing story of Alex Cross, he has admitted defeat. This is indeed a bleak view of human possibilities, and while it is not always true of Cross throughout the series as a whole, it is certainly true of him in these two novels.

ALTERNATIVE READING: THE FRIENDLY READER

Readers of popular fiction—science fiction, mysteries, romances, Westerns, and the like—have definite expectation of each particular genre. Science fiction, no matter what else it does, must have some scientific concept projected into the future and developed beyond its actual contemporary practice. A mystery must have some sort of central question and that question must in some way be resolved at the novel's end. A romance must have two people in love who find resolution of their love at the conclusion. A Western must be set in some recognizable Western setting and must consider the importance of the individual as a causative agent.

Readers who choose popular fiction for their entertainment assume that their anticipations regarding a specific genre will be fulfilled, and they are willing to go some good way in cooperating with the author so that this can happen. They are basically friendly readers. They are more than willing to accept that a murder could occur in a locked room, provided the author gives them some reason—and it doesn't have to be all that plausible a reason—to accept this notion. And they are more than willing to accept that there are superior beings on other planets who come from civilizations far in advance of ours and who long to do nothing more than journey to earth and give us their wisdom. All readers ask in return for such acceptance is that the author go half-way with the reader in creating a scenario by which benevolence on the part of alien races can be accepted, at least for the duration of the story.

Readers are willing to take part in a conspiracy with the author—to pretend that fantasy is reality—because they enjoy the genre or genres involved and because they want to be entertained. The technical term for conspiring with the author in this way is "the willing suspension of disbelief," which is defined as "the willingness [of the reader] to withhold questions about truth, accuracy, or probability in a work. This willingness to suspend doubt makes possible the temporary acceptance of an author's imaginative world" (Holman and Harman 1992, 464).

Every work of fiction ultimately depends on such suspension of disbelief. After all, the reader on some level really does know that the story is only a story and that the characters are only make-believe. Nonetheless, so great is our love of stories and storytelling that we are more than willing to accept the fiction for reality, at least while we are reading the story, if only the author will give us the bare bones of plausibility that will allow us to do this—to enter the world of the author and pretend that it is the real, everyday world.

One interesting way of analyzing a work of fiction—particularly a work of popular fiction, where there are definite audience expectations—is to consider exactly how the author has gone about creating plausibility for the reader. This is especially to the point in a work like *Violets Are Blue,* which focuses on vampires, but it is also to the point in *Roses Are Red,* where the reader is asked to accept that Alex Cross, who is supposedly a superb detective, never suspects that his long-time colleague Kyle Craig is a psychopathic killer. If Cross is so good, why hasn't he caught Craig out long ago? Paradoxically, the reasons for this can be explained specifically in terms of Cross's excellence as a detective; he is the best, and for this reason, only the best can fool him, even temporarily. Craig is Cross's Professor Moriarty, Sherlock Holmes's legendary antagonist, and ultimately, of course, Cross does discover Craig's role in the novel that is serial to this one, *Violets Are Blue*. When he does so Cross establishes himself as the detective who is above all others, because he has caught the villain who is above all others.

Readers of popular fiction have been well-prepared for such a scenario, in which only the best deserve the best. Because readers have come to trust implicitly in Cross, we too do not suspect Craig. We know what Cross knows, we see what he sees, hear what he hears, are privy to his guesses, and furthermore, for any readers who have read earlier novels in the series, we know how good Cross is—he is, after all, the detective who tracked down Gary Soneji, Casanova, and Geoffrey Shafer—if he thinks of Craig as one of the best, then of course we do, too. It's also important in this regard that *Roses Are Red* has three different plot strands, two of which are resolved by the novel's end. The only one left open is the bank robberies and murders planned by the Mastermind, and even though, at the end, Cross still does not know the identity of the Mastermind, the other two plots have been brought to closure, suggesting that, of course, the third one will be, too. This is further foreshadowed by the fact that readers do know Craig is the Mastermind, and we have become so accustomed to Cross knowing more than we do that surely, it can't be long before Cross gets here, too. Thus, instead of seeing this as a failure for Cross, we see it as a foreshadowing of what is to come.

As to the vampires in *Violets Are Blue*, Patterson gives them credibility by being ambiguous as to what is fantasy, what is reality. When, for example, he describes the Church of the Vampire, he tells the reader that it actually is a church, without going into specific detail. Does this mean that it once was a functioning church whose building has been sold or abandoned, and has been taken over by a group of play-acting vampires, or does it mean that it operates as a real church, one dedicated to vampirism? Also, William and Michael, the vampire brothers, and Daniel and Charles, the vampire magicians, are borrowed from popular entertainment; William and Michael mimic the animal training skills of the real-life Las Vegas magicians Siegfried and Roy, as does the superb magical skill of the two fictional vampire magicians. We have seen these people before in one guise or another, and again, the reader is unsure of what is actually supposed to be real here and what is supposed to be make believe. If we accept the incredible feats of Siegfried and Roy, why not go one step further and accept the acts of Daniel and Charles? Settings that add to this blending of real and unreal are Las Vegas, the ultimate make-believe world where we can all go to Egypt by staying at a theme hotel and maybe even become millionaires, and the world of the Goth, an existing subculture of young people who, as Patterson accurately notes, dress all in black and maim themselves with tattoos, body rings, scarification, and the like. What is the line between maiming oneself and maiming others? If I can draw my blood for aesthetic purposes, maybe I can draw yours, too. This careful blurring of what actually occurs in the popular culture with what may occur allows Patterson to create a world of horror that is, at least for the duration of the novel, credible to his readers, who enjoy being scared as much as the next lover of crime fiction. While it is a stretch for a series that focuses primarily on the police procedural to shift its focus to vampires, readers are by this time so familiar with Alex Cross and his track record with psychopaths that they are more than willing to be scared to death by the vampires, too—they know that ultimately Cross will save them.

10

Four Blind Mice (2002)

Four Blind Mice is the eighth Alex Cross novel and it promises to be the last of this particular series since, at its end, Cross has resigned from the Washington, D.C., police force and joined the F.B.I. Fittingly, its title is taken from a nursery rhyme, completing the pattern begun with *Along Came a Spider* (1993), the first of the Alex Cross novels. Certainly a new series may emerge in which Cross is the hero of F.B.I. procedurals. However, his days as a homicide detective in Washington's Southeast end here, as does his partnership with John Sampson, his childhood friend and his long-time partner on the force. This gives *Four Blind Mice* an elegiac quality; Cross and the reader are saying goodbye to an established way of life and venturing into new territory. While readers will be happy that Cross has made a decision about his future (he has been worrying over this through all eight novels, always deciding in the previous seven to stay with the police), they will feel sad that his days with Sampson are (or seem to be) over. Added to this sense of loss is the information that Nana Mama, Cross's grandmother, his conscience and his children's caregiver, is getting older and feeling, for the first time in the series, mortal. On the basis of this novel, major changes are ahead for Alex Cross.

GENRE

All the previous Alex Cross novels fall into the genre of the police procedural, "the subgenre of mystery and detective fiction in which the mystery is solved by the police as part of their professional duties" rather than being solved by a brilliant private detective such as Sherlock Holmes (Kotker 2001, 617). *Four Blind Mice* also shares some aspects of the procedural, particularly its emphasis on how the actual working conditions of policemen impact their home lives; like Cross, they must often be away from spouses and children and their professional obligations are frequently in conflict with their family obligations. As is the established pattern in the series, Cross suffers a good deal of guilt because of this. However, of all the Cross novels, *Four Blind Mice* is closest to a conventional mystery, with its investigation of one crime (a typical procedural has its protagonists investigating more than one crime simultaneously, just as real-life police detectives must do) and the status of its two detectives as outsiders. Here, Cross and Sampson are not working as D.C. policemen but instead as friends of the accused.

The novel begins as that classic of mystery and detective fiction, the wrong man (or wrong woman) novel, made famous in the film of that name, Alfred Hitchcock's *The Wrong Man* (1956), starring Henry Fonda as the unjustly accused. In this subgenre, an innocent person is accused of a crime (usually a capital crime so that a great deal is at stake), and the detective, who may be either an amateur or a professional, takes on the task of proving the innocence of the accused. There is frequently a race-against-the-clock element, as often the accused must be cleared before a set execution date, an element that Patterson includes here. While it is a convention of this particular type of mystery that the innocent person will be cleared, usually at the penultimate moment, in *Four Blind Mice* he is executed by the state in a vividly described, harrowing scene, and the task of his friends Sampson and Cross, still acting as ex-officio detectives, becomes one of determining who has framed him and why.

Four Blind Mice is also a sociological novel, a work that reflects "the nature, function and effect of the society in which characters live" (Holman and Harmon 1992, 448), an element that Patterson frequently uses in his descriptions of crime in Washington, D.C.'s, poor, predominantly African American Southeast neighborhoods. Here, the commentary focuses on the quality of health care for those in Southeast, with a side plot dealing with the military and its culture of protecting its own at the expense of justice for a few. Finally, it is also a romance novel, as all of the Cross novels are, except that in this case the romantic plot features Sampson rather than Cross, and it has a happy ending, unlike Cross's star-crossed relationships.

PLOT DEVELOPMENT

Patterson begins all of the Cross novels with a prologue, and in the case of *Four Blind Mice,* it functions to set up the original situation in a courtroom in North Carolina where a district attorney is describing the murder of four women by Sergeant Ellis Cooper, a decorated war hero who claims that he is innocent. The evidence against him is overwhelming and he is found guilty. Complications immediately follow this prologue when the reader is told, "The real killers had taken a small risk by attending the final day of the trial" (7). They are then identified: Thomas Starkey, Brownley Harris, and Warren Griffin, or the Three Blind Mice. At this point the story line switches to Alex Cross and complications increase as Sampson comes to his home seeking his help; the convicted killer is his friend, someone he served with in Vietnam, and Sampson is certain that he cannot be guilty of this crime. Cross and Sampson set out to clear Cooper, whose execution date is three weeks away (here, Patterson is taking poetic license with timelines; in real life, an execution would take years to work its way through the appeals processes before it actually took place, but it is of course far more dramatic to have a three-week deadline for Cross and Sampson to work against).

When the partners meet with Cooper he says that he was framed, although he is at a loss to know who would do this to him and why. "I don't have an enemy in the world," he says (25). The reader knows who has done this but not why it has been done and so the reader is focused on a "why dunnit," and a "will-the-criminals-be-caught dunnit," while Sampson and Cross are investigating a "whodunnit." This investigation is hampered by the Army, which is unwilling to consider that Cooper might be innocent and which has little use for outside help in the form of two D.C. homicide detectives who don't even work in the jurisdiction of the crime. At this point Cross receives a message telling him that there have been other, similar killings, all by Army men who claimed that they were innocent. Cooper is executed and the puzzle now becomes one of why servicemen with outstanding records are being framed and executed, and on whose orders. As Cross and Sampson continue to investigate, they learn that the roots of the killings lie in a village massacre during the Vietnam War, and that army records have been doctored to cover up atrocities committed there. The executed men were all witnesses to the events and are being framed by the officer who was in charge of the particular mission. He has hired the three killers, each of whom is also an ex-serviceman and served in Vietnam under his command.

In the climax, Cross discovers the identity of the officer and his motive. The officer and two of his colleagues are then murdered in a revenge-killing by a Vietnamese who was once with the Viet Cong and who now controls gangs of Vietnamese youths in America. In the denouement it turns out that no one is innocent; those attempting to cover up the actions of servicemen in Vietnam are killed by equally guilty Vietnamese gang members in a gory finale orchestrated by a leader who is on death row in the United States. And thus ends Cross's last case with the D.C. police; from now on, he will work for the FBI.

CHARACTER DEVELOPMENT

As one would expect, Alex (Alexander Isaiah) Cross is the hero and protagonist of *Four Blind Mice,* although here he is somewhat sketchily drawn and is a static rather than a dynamic character in that he has made a major decision as the novel begins, and at its end, he remains committed to it. In previous novels Patterson has provided detailed background information on Cross: his childhood, his upbringing by his grandmother on the death of his parents, his educational background (he has a Ph.D. in psychology from Johns Hopkins University), the murder of his wife, his subsequent unhappy relationships, his great love for his children, and his guilt at the amount of time he spends away from them. *Four Blind Mice* touches lightly on all of these issues, as though Patterson is assuming (in most cases, correctly) that his reader is already familiar with Cross and has read other novels in the series and now needs only to be reminded of the significant markers in Cross's life. Thus, biographical details are mentioned rather than developed. The weight of the novel, in terms of Cross's character, is on his decision to leave the police and join the FBI, a decision that he has made at the very beginning of the story and that he is at peace with. There is a good deal of emphasis on the fact that this is Cross's last case as a homicide detective, and significantly it isn't even a case for the D.C. police but rather one taken on as a favor for a friend. Cross considers, briefly, going into private practice as a psychologist, but ultimately he stays with his decision to go into the FBI. Sampson, his partner and friend since they were nine years old, tells him, "You talk about leaving the police department; maybe you will. But you like the hunt, Alex" (154).

In the FBI, Cross will be able to continue to hunt, and he will do so with far superior resources than the D.C. police can provide. And when he tells Ron Burns, the FBI director, of his decision, there is a subdued quality of anticipation to his acceptance. Does this mean that there will be no more Alex Cross novels? Ah, this seems most unlikely since Patterson ends the novel with Cross, who is at a Saturday afternoon wedding reception, suddenly noticing that Burns is holding a thick folder and motioning for him. Surely this is a new case for Cross to work on in his new role as FBI investigator and surely we will have many more Cross adventures to follow in this new context.

A significant difference in *Four Blind Mice* from the earlier Cross novels is the emphasis placed on John Sampson. Throughout the novels he has been Cross's friend, partner, and confidant, but he is always clearly the follower to Cross's leader. In *Four Blind Mice,* though, he shares the leadership role with Cross: it is Sampson who initiates the case and who conducts many of the interrogations of witnesses, with Cross taking a back seat to Sampson's superior knowledge of the Army, its procedures, and policies. The reader is given a good deal of information on Sampson's background—more than in any of the previous novels—and learns that his mother was a drug addict and a dealer whose husband abused her before abandoning her and the child. He has always been the ultimate in cool, with his black leather jacket, Wayfarer sunglasses, and an imposing height of six foot nine. He has a reserved manner, and in this novel the reader learns that much of this reserve is based on shyness, "because he'd always been so tall and stood out in every social group" (181). Up to this point he has formed no lasting relationships with women, telling Cross, "My role models on family are bad ones" (155), and so it is delightful to see him fall in love in *Four Blind Mice,* something he does with an air of lightness and joy that is absolutely charming, given his imposing physical presence. Although this is not touched on in the novel, the new relationship for Sampson leaves Cross free to make his decision to join the FBI without having to feel guilt over abandoning his long-time friend and partner, and it helps the series reader to also accept Cross's decision. Sampson, a character the reader has become very fond of over these eight novels, will be all right, he will still have someone to love him. Of the two protagonists, it is Sampson, up until now the minor protagonist, who is the round character here and who is also dynamic, beginning the novel as a cool loner and ending it on his wedding day with his new partner, the diminutive, delightful woman he has just married.

In addition to Cross and Sampson, there are a number of minor protagonists who make cameo appearances. First of these is Sampson's new wife, Billie Houston. He meets her in the course of the investigation—her husband was a serviceman who, like Ellis Cooper, was executed for a crime he did not commit—and at that initial meeting he "liked her immediately. Nothing not to like" (166), preparing the reader for the romance that will follow. While the reader actually knows very little about Houston, she feels like a round character: everything we learn about her is positive, and more important, Sampson fully accepts her. Because we know him so well, she too seems familiar, one of the extended Cross/Sampson family. Also given cameo appearances are Nana Mama, Cross's three children, and a detective from San Francisco, Jamilla Hughes, with whom Cross is in the early stages of a relationship. Of these the emotional focus is on Nana Mama, now 82, who tells Cross, "I never felt like I was seventy, or seventy-five, or even eighty. But Alex, suddenly I feel my age" (192). This strikes an ominous note for both Cross and the reader, since she has been the central figure holding the family together, and while she is in good overall health for her age, she's still 82. Just as Patterson has used *Four Blind Mice* to bring Cross's life as a police detective to closure, so too does he seem to use it to prepare both Cross and the reader for a life without Nana Mama.

If the novel is light on protagonists, it more than makes up for it by having four antagonists, the blind mice of the title. These are three ex-Army rangers who have been close friends since their tour of duty in Vietnam some 30 years before the events of the novel. They get together to drink, party, tell old war stories, and to kill, something they learned to like doing in Vietnam. They are acting here under the direction of the fourth blind mouse, the general who had been their commanding officer and whose goal it is to eliminate the witnesses to an atrocity that happened when they were all together in Vietnam. The three are flat characters in that we see them only in the guise of killers; we have no sense of their dreams and aspirations, nor of what they were like before they went in the service. However, the brutality of their acts is so shocking—at one point, they threaten to peel the skin off a victim—that they fill the screen with horror whenever they appear, taking up all the emotional space available so that the reader prefers knowing as little as possible about them; they are figures of nightmare. They die as they have lived in the novel and there is no sense that any change takes place in their characters; we meet them as vicious killers and they die as vicious killers.

A final, somewhat ambiguous character is an ex-Viet Cong soldier, Tran Van Luu, now in prison for life. He too is a vicious killer and he is a figure who must have great power, since he can arrange the revenge killing of the fourth blind mouse from his cell on death row. His ambiguity lies in the fact that he helps Cross to discover the killers and their motives and ultimately is responsible for saving Cross's life. In this respect, he acts as a protagonist, although in all other respects, he is a source of violence and could easily be developed into one of Patterson's psychopathic killers on the model of Gary Soneji and Thomas Pierce. As with the four blind mice, he is a flat character whose only outstanding quality is that of evil, but in his case, the roots of his evil are at least understandable; his entire family was slaughtered by renegade American soldiers and he has since sought revenge for what he describes as the destruction of "an entire country, a culture" (357).

SETTING

As noted in Chapter 3, setting refers to both the natural and the artificial scenery in which the characters in a work exist and the story takes place. Natural setting refers to those elements of setting that exist in the natural world (mountains, streams, forests, the weather, and so on). Artificial setting refers to those elements that are man-made (buildings and furniture, for example). Artificial setting also includes the clothes an author dresses his or her characters in.

Setting can be used to show what a character is like (we learn a lot about people from how they dress and what kind of houses they live in), to create a sense of atmosphere (a storm about to strike is a standard way of creating an atmosphere suggesting that something terrible is about to happen), and even to show character motivation (there may be something in the setting, either natural or artificial, that causes a character to act in a particular way). A standard way of analyzing setting is to consider the impact of natural and artificial settings on a particular work. As a general rule, Patterson is a writer whose primary emphasis is on plot development, and in most of his work, setting serves as a backdrop for plot rather than a key element in and of itself. However, in *Four Blind Mice* Patterson exploits the possibilities of setting to add to both plot and character. This is most apparent in the descriptions of prisons in this novel. When Cross and Sampson visit Ellis Cooper, we are told that "the security housing unit there was like a prison within a prison" and that it is surrounded by "razor-sharp wire fences and a deadly electronic barrier; armed guards were in all the watchtowers" (22). It is a very quiet place with "hundreds of controlled steel gates." Inmates cannot move outside of their cells "without handcuffs, leg irons, and security guards," (23) and the normally unflappable Sampson says of the prison, "Scary place." Cross thinks that he has never seen him look so unhappy, and adds, "I didn't much like being at Central Prison either" (22). For these two hardened detectives to find the prison so ominous emphasizes the seriousness of Cooper's situation and foreshadows the fact that he cannot escape it.

A second prison setting is the maximum security unit in Colorado. Here, the interview room consists of a table and two chairs, all of them bolted to the floor, and the prisoner is accompanied by three guards wearing body armor and protective gloves, a terrifying image in and of itself. One effect of this description is to make the prisoner, in this case Tran Van Luu, seem so dangerous that it is more than believable that he could, even from this prison, be the mastermind of criminal gangs. Together, these two prison settings combine to create an image of inescapable violence.

Patterson also uses artificial setting in *Four Blind Mice* as ironic commentary in descriptions such as that of Thomas Starkey's home. Starkey, a vicious killer, lives in a handsome brick house with shutters and white trim, a house that most Americans envision when they think of owning a dream home. It's set in a neighborhood that Starkey describes as being made up of "decent people in all these houses up and down the street" (280), highlighting by this description Starkey's very lack of decency.

A final example of artificial setting, this time used to foreshadow events, is the description of the hotel room where Jamilla Hughes and Cross stay. Designed to resemble a log cabin, it is warm, cozy, and home-like, perhaps to indicate the future that lies before them and that will be worked out in a subsequent novel.

As with artificial setting, the natural setting of *Four Blind Mice* is used to both terrify and foreshadow. There is a description of an eerie, scary, ancient forest that feels straight out of a Grimm's fairy tale. Surely this a place where bad things happen and so it is most fitting that it is the hideaway cabin of Starkey and his two assistants, a place where they kill for amusement. In contrast, there are wonderful descriptions of the Jersey shore with its rolling dunes and great sweep of ocean. This is the home of Billie Houston, and when Sampson first meets her, it is at a beach house named Paradise Found. For Sampson, the experience of the ocean is indeed like being in paradise, and this suggests to readers that the changes coming into his life with the loss of Cross as a partner and the gain of Billie as a wife will be equally wonderful, something we want to believe because we have become fond of Sampson and we do not wish to see him abandoned and alone. Here, the idyllic ocean setting strongly suggests that Sampson will be more than all right and definitely not alone.

POINT OF VIEW

As outlined in previous chapters, James Patterson typically uses two points of view in the novels in the Alex Cross series, and *Four Blind Mice* is no exception. Just as he has done in the previous Cross novels, Patterson uses first person, the "I" voice, for those chapters that center on Cross, and third person omniscient, in which an unknown narrator who can see what all the characters are doing and thinking tells the story, for those chapters centering on other characters. First person, using the "I" voice from the point of view of Cross, causes the reader to identify with Cross, and, in effect, to become an investigator along with him. When Cross gathers evidence and that evidence is shared with the reader, the reader too becomes a detective, seeking to find the solution by the same means as Cross. One of the delights of mystery and detective fiction for many readers is to work out the solution to the crime in the same manner as the detective does, and the use of first person allows the reader to do precisely this.

The sections of the story told in third person omniscient are an effective way of showing the reader those elements of plot and character that Cross cannot be privy to, either because he is not in the mind of a particular character or because he is not part of a particular scene and therefore cannot act as a witness to it. Thus, seeing Sampson's developing romance from the third person point of view emphasizes its almost magical quality wherein he goes to an enchanted place (the Eden-like ocean and coast of New Jersey) and meets Billie Houston, a diminutive princess with whom it seems entirely possible that he will live happily ever after. While this scene could be told from Sampson's point of view, it is unlikely that the very reserved, shy Sampson would express himself in such an open manner and so the use of the omniscient point of view allows the reader to experience the relationship as Sampson does, despite his reticence. By the same token, if Cross were to report to the reader on this romance from his first person perspective, his very astonishment over Sampson's falling in love would undermine the fairy-tale ending; the reader would be focusing on "Can this be true?" rather than on "How wonderful for Sampson."

Third person is equally convincing in its depiction of the killers, the blind mice of the title, because of its ability to show the psychotic delight they take in the act of killing. They abduct a young woman for fun and then kill her, after a macabre chase through the woods in which they glory in their hunting abilities. There is no reason to kill her—she is not one of the designated victims they've been hired to eliminate, she's just someone who happens along, the classic example of the innocent person in the wrong place at the wrong time—but they seize this opportunity for what is to them a little light entertainment. Since Cross is not in the scene, he would be unable to show the reader this bizarre aspect of the killers, an aspect that helps the reader to understand how deranged they are despite their seeming middle-class American normalcy. This technique of showing the killers from a perspective other than Cross's is used a number of times throughout the novel and adds to its overall horror—when we see them as they see themselves, we shudder.

THEMATIC ISSUES

As noted in the opening to this chapter, *Four Blind Mice* is very much a novel of change, and one major theme is that such change is inevitable, outside of our control. However, what is in our control is how we respond to change: those who remain trapped in the past are condemned to repeat it over and over again, with no resolution, whereas those who accept it are able to move on and, ultimately, embrace life. This theme applies to all of the major characters, both protagonists and antagonists. It can be seen in Alex Cross's decision to leave the police and join the FBI. For the past few years he has been repeating his same routines in a job that, although he loves it for the thrill of the hunt and for the fact that as a policeman, he sometimes really does make a difference in the world, that he sometimes does eliminate evil by capturing psychopathic killers such as Gary Soneji and Kyle Craig, the job itself no longer fits the personal world he lives in. Radical change entered that world with the random killing of his wife, and he is now a single parent with three growing children who need care and attention. Their only other caregiver is an 82-year-old woman, and while she is strong and energetic, she is still 82 and the physical demands of running this household are simply becoming too much for her. Cross is able to give her little help since his job as policeman involves long hours, an uncertain schedule, and much time spent away from home. He has known for some time that the demands of the job and the demands of his home life are incompatible, and finally, in *Four Blind Mice,* he makes the choice to leave the police and join the FBI, where he will be able to make much better use of his training as a psychologist and, more important, have a predictable schedule that will allow him to take on more of the responsibility of parenting his children. As soon as he makes this decision, there is a sense of closure; he has accepted the reality of his changed world and is creating a new reality for himself.

Another major character who chooses to leave his past and move into a new reality is John Sampson, Cross's long-time police partner. He is essentially doing the opposite of what Cross is doing; where Cross is changing professions, Sampson is changing his personal world. He comes from a dysfunctional inner-city background with a mother who was a prostitute and drug addict and a father who was also a drug addict and who abandoned the family. Both parents were abusive to Sampson and to one another, and this has remained his role model for how families interact with one another. For this reason, he has always avoided any long-term commitments with women, and at the same time, he is becoming less and less content with his personal life. When he goes to the Jersey shore, it is as though he has a revelation about life and the possibilities it offers him. He experiences the ocean as something new, almost another world, one that he just this moment has become aware of. He thinks that "recently his days on the job in D.C. seemed tougher and more gruesome than usual" but now, on this beach, he does not see his life this way, "and it had happened instantly. He felt that he could hear and see things with unusual clarity" (165). He is at the ocean to question Billie Houston, whose husband was falsely accused, framed, and executed two years previously in what was a set-up by the blind mice killers, and as soon as he meets her, she too becomes part of the enchanted ocean setting. Cautious, wary Sampson likes her immediately. He accepts her world and, returning to it later in the novel, he thinks how glad he is to be there again, that it's a long way from D.C. and the murders he has been investigating. They make love and Sampson realizes that he is at peace "for the first time in years. Maybe ever" (252). When, at the end of the novel, Sampson marries Billie, it is as though he is choosing the future over the past, a future that has oceans and beaches in it as opposed to a past limited to inner-city decay and crime. While the decay and crime will still be a part of his world, they will only be a part: from now on, the world will contain oceans, beaches, and peacefulness, too.

Nana Mama is another example of the inevitability of change in this novel, and of someone accepting that change and going on with her life. She has long been one of the key characters of the Cross series, acting as his conscience and as a voice of morality and personal strength within a world in which such qualities can be rare. She has raised Cross, helped to raise Sampson, and now is raising Cross's three children. An intelligent, articulate woman, she takes on the bigots of the world, confronting racism, prejudice, and injustice wherever she meets them. Time is catching up with her, though, and she knows it. Nonetheless, she says, "I'm taking care of myself so far, and I plan to keep doing it" (193). She is a superb example of a character who accepts the changes in her life; where she might be attempting to still live in the past, she is instead choosing to live in the present, with the limitations that imposes on her. She helps the reader to believe that Cross and his family will carry on without her when the time comes because of the fine example she has set for them in terms of accepting life.

The antagonists of the novel are, without exception, characters who are unable to leave the past and move on. Starkey, Harris, and Griffin, three of the blind mice of the title, continue to live in the 1960s. They call one another boys, and their lives are still dominated by their experiences as young soldiers (indeed, boys) in Vietnam. They play the same songs, eat the same food, use the same military terminology they used then, speak pidgin Vietnamese and conceptualize their roles as killers in terms of their battle experiences in Vietnam. When a girl they are terrorizing asks them why they are doing this to her, Starkey answers, "This is a game we learned a long time ago" (70). While the realities of war are such that they may have needed to frame them in terms of games in order to deal with them at the time, the war has long been over, and, like thousands of other young men who went through these same experiences, the three had the choice of accepting that it is behind them and moving on to the present they now live in. Instead, they remain locked in the past and its world of violence and terror.

Another antagonist locked in the past is the ex-Vietnamese scout Tran Van Luu, who has dedicated himself to seeking revenge against the American soldiers responsible for the deaths of his family and the people of his village. Although he has lived in the United States for almost two decades, he sees himself as still being in a war. He has become the leader of a powerful Vietnamese gang that he has modeled on the social structure of his old village, and he continues to control the gang even though he is now on death row. For him, then, the result of living in the past has been a continuation of violence and it seems certain to end in yet greater violence, his execution by the state. Ironically, this execution will be carried out by the representatives of those he seeks vengeance against.

Overall, then, only those characters in the novel who are open to change, whether it is the positive change of Cross and Sampson or the negative change of Nana Mama, succeed in taking control of their lives, while the remaining characters' lives are controlled by a bitter past.

ALTERNATIVE READING: AUTHORIAL TECHNIQUES

A difficult task that James Patterson has set for himself in *Four Blind Mice* is that of treating separation and death in such a way that they are bearable for the reader. A particularly good example of this is the execution of Ellis Cooper, the Army sergeant who has been framed for the murder of three women. As noted earlier in this chapter, when Cooper is introduced, readers fully expect to find themselves in the midst of a wrong man plot, where suspense consists of how the innocent victim will be freed. Such freeing is a convention of this plot structure and therefore the reader fully expects it in this story, too. There is, as noted, usually an element of a race against the clock involved in wrong man plots, with the accused being released at the penultimate moment. Thus, following convention, up until the last seconds before his execution the reader expects to see Cooper miraculously saved in some way. This expectation is reinforced by the fact that it is Alex Cross and John Sampson who have come to his rescue, and we are accustomed to their succeeding when they take on a case. However, this time it doesn't happen; they fail, the clock runs out, and Cooper is executed. Oddly enough, the execution does not feel like a failure to readers, and it is interesting to analyze the methods Patterson uses so that readers accept the death of this sympathetic character, a task made particularly difficult for Patterson by the fact that Sampson, who knows Cooper almost as well as he knows Cross, is convinced of his innocence.

One technique that serves Patterson well in our acceptance of the death is the ultimate response of Cooper to his situation. First of all the reader is struck by Cooper's ability to empathize with the women who have been killed. When he is maintaining his innocence, he says that he didn't kill "any of those poor women" (6) and his seeing them in this light, that is, his ability to feel sorry for them at the same time that he himself is being falsely accused, suggests a grandeur of spirit. This is reinforced by his reaction when Sampson and Cross visit him. He says that the visit is the best thing that has happened to him in some good time, and having a man on death row respond with such evident pleasure to the presence of a friend who is unable to help him is difficult indeed to imagine. It requires a largeness of spirit to see beyond one's own needs and fears to the intentions of others. Cooper also has a quality of humility about him. He was a sergeant when Sampson first met him years ago and he remains a sergeant today, a man who has reached the limits of his potential and who accepts without any bitterness that he has done so. This ability to accept his life and to take pleasure in circumstances with little pleasure to offer causes readers to become fond of Cooper and to take him at his own estimate. For this reason, when he assures Sampson and Cross that they have done everything anyone could have done and that the "Deck was stacked against us" (103), we respect his response and it becomes our own. Cross says of Cooper, "He seemed strangely at peace to me" (104) and this causes readers to be at peace with his fate, too. Thus, instead of experiencing the death of Cooper as a failure of Cross and Sampson, we experience it as closure.

Patterson uses much the same technique in presenting Nana Mama's age and mortality to the reader. When she tells Cross that she is 82 and coming now to feel her age, it is as though she is asserting her right to be old and, in doing so, continuing to exert control over her life. Because we admire her, we admire her choices, and so, as with Ellis Cooper, there is a sense of closure in her acceptance that is ultimately comforting to the reader—we have been forewarned of her death and will be able to acknowledge it when it comes. In this way, then, Patterson has created character development techniques allowing readers to accept consequences that under most circumstances would go against our natural bias.

11

1st to Die (2001)

With *1st to Die,* James Patterson introduces what promises to be a new series, one focusing on the Women's Murder Club, a group made up of an inspector with the San Francisco Police Department, the chief medical examiner for San Francisco, a reporter for a major San Francisco newspaper, and an assistant District Attorney for San Francisco. While all of these women have their individual professions, they meet with one another outside of their regular work hours to discuss cases and to act as both a professional and a private support group for one another. In this, they are reminiscent of the first mysteries written for girls, beginning with such early series as The Motor Girls (1910) and The Motor Maids (1912), whose protagonists were groups of girls who "exhibited uncommon bravery and maturity . . . and uncovered crucial clues, performing amazing rescues, or revealing uncanny intuition" (Mason 1995, 11). Because they could drive, these girls had independence and mobility and a strong argument can be made that they were the first liberated female detectives. They morph into Nancy Drew (introduced in the 1930s), whose "blue car," Bobbie Ann Mason says, "carried her into more dangerous situations than usually graced the pages of girls' books." Mason also notes that in the Drew series "there was a deliberate focus on an unusually strong heroine, far more accomplished and independent than any of her predecessors.

[She] was more liberated than girls had dared imagine—as free and self-possessed as any adult" (1995, 16). If one were to construct an evolutionary scale of proto-feminist detectives, it could well show Nancy Drew developing into the character of Effie Perrine, Sam Spade's brave and loyal secretary in *The Maltese Falcon* (1930), and she in turn developing into P. D. James's Cordelia Gray (*An Unsuitable Job for a Woman*, 1972). Gray would be followed by Thomas Harris's FBI agent-in-training Clarice Starling (*The Silence of the Lambs*, 1988). With Clarice, the evolution would be complete; the girl-into-woman detective is born, equal in all ways to her male counterparts. And while Effie Perrine and Cordelia Gray are essentially loners, Clarice Starling has a supportive relationship with another female student at the FBI academy, perhaps a forerunner of the relationships Patterson develops for his group in *1st to Die.*

Traditionally, murder clubs have been masculine groups who have met to tell one another murder stories and compete with one another to solve the puzzles. Sometimes, the narrator of the story knows the answers, and at others, the group arrives at the answers (usually after many highly plausible, incorrect solutions), as in John Dickson Carr's *He Who Whispers* (1946). Anthony Lejeune, writing in *The Oxford Companion to Crime and Mystery Writing*, notes that "Clubmen everywhere may frown on murder theoretically and deplore it on their own premises, but in fiction and in fact they love talking about it" (1999, 78). The actual site for Women's Murder Club meetings in *1st to Die* is a public restaurant rather than a private club, but the same conventions apply to it as to the traditional clubs; it is the site of privacy and camaraderie. With their masculine connotations, clubs in general became somewhat passé in mystery writing in the midst of the 1970s feminist revolution in politics and criticism. However, perhaps Patterson has begun a trend toward bringing them back with his new club series focusing on women.

GENRE

1st to Die combines four popular genres: that of the girl detectives, that of the psychopathic killer, in which a selected group of people is targeted and killed in vicious ways not because of any harm they have done to the murderer but as a result of the murderer's uncontrollable rage to kill, the classic detective story, in which a murder is committed and the detective protagonist is charged with discovering who the murderer is and bringing him or her to justice, and the romance novel, defined by Rosenberg and Herald as "true love triumphant against all odds" (1991, 143). In *1st to*

Die, however, as in most of the other Patterson books covered here, true love turns out to be not so triumphant after all.

PLOT DEVELOPMENT

In all of his novels, Patterson has established a pattern of opening with a prologue, although the prologue in *1st to Die* begins after the initial murders have taken place. This makes it atypical Patterson since it acts as a flashback rather than as his usual foreshadowing device, and as such it retrospectively introduces the protagonist, her support group (to be known as the Women's Murder Club), her personal sense of despair, and the nature of the crime itself. All of these elements are only briefly alluded to, acting as teasers that entice the reader to page on for more details. The novel then shifts its focus to David and Melanie Brandt, murdered while on their honeymoon in San Francisco. This pair becomes the first of what will be known throughout the novel as "The Honeymoon Murders" and the fact that the bride is sexually violated after death puts the narrative squarely in the psycho-killer genre. Besides the post-mortem violation, another oddity of the killing is that the victims' wedding rings are removed by the killer, although all of their clothes and jewelry are left intact. The second killing in the series targets two honeymooners who are murdered in a limousine on the night of their wedding, and once again, there has been a post-mortem sexual attack on the bride, with the same pattern of only the wedding rings being taken.

While both of these killings are set on the West Coast, the third murder takes place in Cleveland. Again, the rings are removed and the bride violated. At this point, Lindsay Boxer, an inspector with the San Francisco Police Department who has been assigned the honeymoon cases, determines, through fine detective work, that the killer is in all probability the successful author Nicholas Jenks, a man whose first (unpublished) novel has as its central theme the killing of brides and grooms. Of course, all dedicated readers of James Patterson novels know very well by now that, if nothing else, they are to distrust the obvious, and sure enough, it turns out that Jenks is not the killer after all. Instead, his second wife, Chessy, has committed the crimes, acting on his orders.

Much of the plot of *1st to Die* can be analyzed as a classic mystery, with an original situation, complications, a crisis or climax, and a denouement. Following this type of analysis, the original situation is the world of the work of fiction before something happens to disrupt it. In *1st to Die,* this is the routine, day-to-day life in upper middle-class San Francisco, a world that includes elegant social affairs such as society marriages of the young and beautiful, personified by the newlyweds David and Melanie, who are in an elegant hotel room, sipping champagne and celebrating their brand-new marriage, when the first complication occurs.

Complications in fiction are something out of the ordinary, something that the characters must deal with in some way. Often, there is an initial major complication that puts into play a whole series of further complications, and *1st to Die* follows this pattern with the brutal murders of David and Melanie in their honeymoon hotel room. These murders are followed by those of a newlywed couple in Northern California. Here, one of the most damaging events that can happen during a police investigation occurs; a reporter happens to be on the scene and recognizes the significance of this second killing, with its similarities to the earlier one. Since the first murder was in San Francisco, the case was assigned to Lindsay Boxer, a homicide investigator with the San Francisco police, and now, called in on the second murder, she needs to gain the reporter's allegiance so that the investigation is not compromised by the early release of information. She does this by bonding with the reporter, the novice Cindy Thomas, promising to trade information for silence so that Thomas will have an early scoop only when Boxer authorizes it. As it turns out, Thomas takes on a significant role in the investigation, using her reporter's research skills to gather information.

Boxer's other significant source of both information and support is Claire Washburn, San Francisco's chief medical examiner. She has been Boxer's close friend for years, and she, Thomas, and Boxer now form the nucleus of the Women's Murder Club, a group that meets after work and discusses the progress of the case, feeding off one another's ideas and expertise. They are subsequently joined by Jill Bernhardt, an assistant D.A. to whom the case is assigned. At this point a third murder occurs, this time of a newlywed couple in Ohio. Meanwhile, the official investigation of the crime continues in the traditional manner, with the tracking and connecting of clues, such as the fact that all the brides bought their gowns at the same elegant store in San Francisco. Simultaneously, complications continue along another plot strand (Patterson is well known for his multiple plots, and *1st* is no exception) with Boxer's discovery that she has aplastic anemia, a potentially fatal blood disease, so that two dramas are now unfolding: the murders and the outcome of Boxer's illness. This is added to when Boxer falls in love with her new partner, Chris Raleigh, creating a classic romantic plot with the central question, "Will true love find a way?"

As the investigation unfolds the women discover that the author Nicholas Jenks, a famous screen writer and a sexual sadist, had some years ago written an unpublished novel, *Always a Bridesmaid,* describing in detail the murders that have now been committed. Jenks is arrested for the killings and *1st to Die* would seem to have reached its climax or emotional high point, but the arrest turns out to be yet another complication rather than a solution; Jenks cannot be the murderer because he is left-handed and the killer was indisputably right-handed. In the actual climax, Jenks's wife Chessy is identified as the murderer and is killed in a shoot-out with Boxer.

In the denouement, or wrapping up of the novel, the reader learns that Chessy was acting on Jenks's orders and under his direction. He comes after Boxer, intending to kill her, and she shoots and kills him instead. Thus, all the villains are neatly disposed of, the Women's Murder Club is born, Boxer's anemia is under control, but there is no happy ending for the romance; Chris dies in the shoot-out with Chessy and so the answer to this final sub-plot strand is that, at least in *1st to Die,* true love does not find a way.

CHARACTER DEVELOPMENT

Lindsay Boxer is the protagonist of *1st to Die,* and she is the most well-rounded of the characters in the novel in that we have the most information on her background and motivations. Her mother is dead and her father, also a policeman, left the family when Boxer was 13. She majored in sociology in college and then joined the police department. Now 34 years old, she has been the lead homicide investigator with the San Francisco police department for six years, a position at which she excels. Boxer attributes her success in the department to the fact that she can be both logical and highly emotional, something that she says is an unusual combination in a homicide detective. Boxer has been married once, to an up-and-coming corporate lawyer who left her. The reasons for his leaving are unclear; he is a hazy figure whose only function in the story is to show that Lindsay has had negative romantic experiences and is therefore leery of forming attachments. She says of herself that she hates living alone and, at the same time, is "afraid to be with somebody again. What if he suddenly stopped loving me?" (41). It is this quality that makes the Women's Murder Club so important to her. Once she begins meeting with the other members she says, "I felt something happening, something that hadn't happened in a long time, that I desperately needed. I felt connected" (124).

This in turn becomes a believable motivation for why a professional policeman might do something so unprofessional as to form a private investigating group. While it would probably never happen in reality, it is believable in the context of the novel, given the character Patterson has developed for Boxer. It is noteworthy that Boxer has absolute trust in this women's group, in contrast to her lack of trust in her ability to form lasting romantic relationships with men. Finally, as the story of the murders progresses, the reader simultaneously follows the progress of Boxer's disease, rejoicing with her when she learns that she is cured. Boxer is a dynamic character in that she begins the novel doubting in her ability to form romantic relationships and ends it having done exactly that, although the man in question is killed at the conclusion of the story. Nonetheless, she now knows that such a relationship is a possibility for her, knowledge she lacked when the story began.

The other three women in the Women's Murder Club, Cindy Thomas, Claire Washburn, and Jill Bernhardt, are all sketched in rather than fully developed, with greatest attention paid to Thomas and Washburn. Thomas is a 29-year-old reporter who is just beginning her professional life when, by luck, she is assigned to the Honeymoon Murders (she's the only person available). This is her first big story and in her pursuit of it she proves herself to be intelligent, tenacious, and feisty. She's a good researcher, as a journalist must be, and this quality makes it credible to the reader that Boxer might indeed include her in the women's murder group. Thomas knows how to ask questions and how to get answers, and as a journalist, she has wide access to people without the legal restrictions that constrain Boxer as a police official. She is a static character, the same eager young journalist at the end as she was at the beginning, although given her access to confidential police sources, her career is definitely more promising than when she was first introduced.

Claire Washburn, the San Francisco medical examiner who is the third member of the Women's Murder Club, is Boxer's best friend, although how the friendship came about is left open. Of the four women in the club she is the only one who has children and she sees herself as "blessed and radiant" because "she had made it up from a tough, mostly black neighborhood in San Francisco to become a doctor. Because she was loved. Because she was taught to give love" (147). Washburn is African American and she is another example of Patterson's inclusion of positive African American role models in his novels, following such memorable characters as Jimmie Horn in *The Thomas Berryman Number* and Alex Cross in the novels in that series. Like Thomas, Washburn is lightly sketched in and remains a static character throughout in that she ends the novel as she began it. Her inclusion in the group is the most understandable of the four women, given her professional role in the police department and the interaction that she and Boxer would inevitably have as a result of this.

Finally, the fourth member of the Women's Murder Club is Jill Bernhardt, a 34-year-old assistant district attorney who is elegant, beautifully dressed, and a sharp-edged high-achiever. Like Washburn, she is also married although she lacks Washburn's sense of contentment, and Boxer says of her that although her life has all the trappings of success, "there seemed to be something missing" (252). Perhaps it is this lack that explains her willingness to participate in the group since, as with Boxer, it is an unlikely role for a woman in her professional position to take on, given the potential for conflict between her responsibilities as district attorney and her sharing of privileged information with these close friends. Like Thomas and Washburn, Bernhardt is also a static figure, ending the novel as she has begun it.

The final protagonist in *1st to Die* is Chris Raleigh, a sometime-policeman who is now a Community Action liaison with the mayor's office and who is assigned to work with Boxer on the high-profile honeymoon killer case. Like her, he is also divorced and the two are immediately attracted to one another. This attraction develops and Boxer discovers that she can have a good relationship with a man despite her previous failures, at which point Raleigh is killed in a shootout. (The title, *1st to Die,* refers to his death; Boxer, with her disease, had assumed that she would be the first to die, but ironically Raleigh rather than Boxer earns that dubious honor.) Raleigh is basically a stock character, the handsome, caring, sensitive man whom most women hope one day to meet and who perhaps is too good to be true, as indicated by his death. Boxer finds Mr. Right, and in the next breath, he's gone. His primary function is to show that Boxer, now able to have positive relationships with men, has come through a dark place in her personal life, both in terms of her illness and of her emotions.

There are two antagonists in *1st to Die,* both of whom act in concert. Of these the most significant is Nicholas Jenks who, although he does not commit the murders, directs them and in this way is responsible for them. Jenks is a bestselling author and a handsome, famous national figure. He is also a sexual sadist of whom his first wife says, "He preys on weakness" (276). He is an obsessive, and Boxer speculates that the murders may be being committed so that Jenks can use the information to see what murdering someone is like and so write better books. Clearly, he is another of

Patterson's sick, twisted psychopaths and he is perhaps the least attractive of all of them since no rationale is given for his behavior unlike, say, that of Gary Soneji of *Along Came a Spider*, whose abuse as a child helps explain the adult he became. Jenks comes from a middle-class family and is well educated. The only hints we have of the roots of his viciousness are that his father was also a sexual sadist, and that as a boy Jenks was aware of how this played out in his parents' marriage. He must be a charismatic figure because both his first and second wives were in turn mesmerized by him; Joanna, the first wife, says to Boxer, "I know he's capable of completely debasing another human being. . . . He preys on weakness. . . . But let me tell you the worst thing, the very worst. He left me, Inspector. I didn't leave him" (275–76). Jenks's power over his second wife, Chessy, is even greater since she has actually committed the murders, with their ugly after-death sexual mutilations, and has done so under his direction. "We were *living out* the plot of a novel," Jenks tells Boxer, a novel of which Jenks is the proud author (422; italics in original). He is such a monstrous creature that he seems well-rounded despite the little the reader actually knows about him—the few details given are so overwhelming as to block out any empty spaces in his characterization. As with most of the other characters in this novel he is also static, ending it in the same ugly way he began it, a man who revels in pain and death. When, at the very end, Boxer kills him, there is a strong feeling that the world has been rid of a vicious evil.

The remaining antagonist is the murderer Chessy Jenks, Nicholas Jenks's second wife. She, too, is a flat character given that we know little of her background and less of Jenks's attraction for her. We know that she is capable of violence, given the six murders she commits, and that she is a superb actor who can convincingly take on the role of a man since for much of the novel she appears as Phillip Campbell, a fictional character of Jenks's who commits on paper the murders Chrissy carries out in real life. How she became involved with Jenks and why she follows his orders is never made clear; we accept her as an antagonist not so much for the believability of her motivation as for the fascination of the details about how she takes on the masculine role of the killer and makes it credible. She also adds a favorite plot strand of Patterson's to the novel by confusing the issue of who exactly the villain is. For most of the book it seems to be Phillip Campbell and it is typical of Patterson to misdirect the reader in this way: the killer is X (Campbell); no, the killer is Y (Nicholas Jenks); wait, no, the killer is Z (Chessy Jenks). Such misdirection has been characteristic of Patterson's work since his first novel, *The Thomas Berryman*

Number, and with the male impersonation here, he adds another gloss to a well-established formula.

SETTING

Setting nearly always plays a small role in James Patterson's novels, with the emphasis being on plot. In some novels he uses artificial or man-made setting to establish scenes of gothic horror (this is especially true of *Along Came a Spider,* which conjures up images of being buried alive at an abandoned farm). In the Cross series as a whole, setting contributes to the conventions of the police procedural genre by establishing that the police are indeed overworked and underpaid and that they live modestly, at best. In most of these Cross novels, setting also helps to create a sociological sub-text highlighting the contrast between the way the powerful establishment figures of Washington, D.C., live and the way the poor in that same city live. Natural setting is usually less significant to Patterson, although when he does employ it, it is almost always for the sake of irony: characters who seem to inhabit paradise find themselves, one way or another, inhabiting hell.

The major settings in *1st to Die* are the post-wedding scenes at which the murders take place. The first murder opens in the San Francisco Grand Hyatt's Mandarin Suite with its spectacular views of the Golden Gate Bridge. Here, as the newlyweds drink champagne and luxuriate in their surroundings, a killer enters, turning an enchanted space into a scene of carnage. Similarly, the second pair of killings takes place at an elegant spa in the mountains, a place where people go to escape the banality of everyday life; instead, they find murder. The third site is perhaps the most ironic of all; the bride and groom have chosen the Rock 'n' Roll Hall of Fame for their wedding reception, a place associated with the trappings and euphoria of youth rather than the terror and obscenity of death. When they are killed here, it is as though murder were introduced into Disneyland—it just isn't supposed to happen here. This contrast between setting and events heightens the horror of the actual murders and is an excellent example of the way in which setting can contribute to plot and character: only someone very twisted would set murder in such surroundings.

POINT OF VIEW

James Patterson's favored point of view in the Cross series and now in this first of the Women's Murder Club series is a double point of view:

first person for his protagonists, Alex Cross in that series and now Lindsey Boxer in this one, and third person omniscient for all other characters (see Chapter 3 for a fuller discussion of point of view). When he is writing in first person, the story is told using the "I" voice, a technical device that causes the reader to identify with the narrator. It is an intimate voice that blurs the distinction between narrator and reader so that when the narrator is puzzled, the reader is also puzzled; when the narrator is angry, the reader understands the source of the anger; and when the narrator is betrayed, the reader too feels betrayed, having experienced events as the narrator has. This is particularly effective in *1st to Die* with respect to Boxer's illness; she is a young, healthy woman who takes decent care of her body and now it has turned on her. Through the use of the "I" voice the reader can well understand Boxer's reluctance to reach out and tell others about what is happening to her; if she keeps it to herself, perhaps it won't really be true. Nearly everyone has experienced this sort of denial and, with the use of the "I" voice, can relate to resorting to the same unsuccessful techniques in an attempt to ward off the unbearable.

When Patterson shifts to third person omniscient, in which an unidentified omniscient narrator who can see into the minds of all the characters tells the tale, he opens up the novel to the charismatic power of his major antagonist, Jenks. As noted before, Jenks is one of Patterson's scummiest villains, a novelist so enamored of his own work that he brings it to life in the real world. Through the use of the third person the reader sees how despicable he is and, at the same time, marvels at the power he has over both his wife and his ex-wife. It is also a very effective point of view in its ability to mislead the reader. Because the reader seems to be in the mind of the killer, that killer seems to be known to be a man named Phillip Campbell. However, Patterson has once again performed a sleight-of-hand trick in which what is known turns out to be false, and there really is no such person as Phillip Campbell. Had the novel been told in first person throughout, the double layer of deception would have been lost, since the focus would have been on the search for a villain who was always seen through the prism of the first person narrator. The fact that this villain was made up of two personas would not be known until the end of the novel, eliminating a strand of mystery and deception that adds to the puzzle.

THEMATIC ISSUES

Overall, even though the killer is himself killed and the protagonist recovers from a potentially fatal illness, the underlying message in *1st to*

Die is a bleak one that can be stated as, "In this life, there are no certainties. The best one can do is accept life and continue to try again in the knowledge that most of the time, happy endings will elude us."

This message is particularly apparent in the romantic relationships in the novel. Lindsay Boxer has been married to a corporate lawyer who left her, for reasons that are never clear to her, and the very ambiguity of the motive emphasizes lack of control over one's fate. If she has no idea why he left, then she has no control over it; if she doesn't know what she could have done, then by extension nothing she could do would change the outcome. Chris Raleigh, the partner Boxer falls in love with, is himself divorced, and although at first he looks like he will be the happy, romantic ending most readers would want for Boxer, he is killed in a shooting that, again, she cannot control. Nicholas Jenks has been married twice and in both cases his wives were demeaned and exploited by him, to the point that he completely dominated them and they were incapable of leaving him. Jill Bernhardt is also married, although the marriage seems a distant one (her husband reminds the reader of Boxer's husband, the lawyer who left her for unknown reasons), and it is difficult to look at it as an advertisement for the successful marriage. Cindy Thomas, the baby of the group, has no romantic involvements, leaving Claire Washburn, the final member of the Women's Murder Club, as the only one with a happy relationship; she and her husband are very supportive of one another and clearly add to the richness of each other's lives.

Out of six romantic relationships, only one succeeds in this novel, and it is a testament to Patterson's belief in the possibility of love that it is this sole relationship that is ultimately the most believable, suggesting that if we continue to strive for happiness, there is at least a chance that we can achieve it, rare though it may be.

ALTERNATIVE READING: A FEMINIST ANALYSIS

A sociological analysis of literature is one that looks at a given work from the perspective of the effects of its society on the lives of the characters within the work. A specialized form of sociological analysis is feminist analysis, in which a piece of literature is studied for what it reveals about the status of women within its world. This type of analysis derives from feminism as a social movement, beginning with Mary Wollstonecraft's *A Vindication of the Rights of Women* (1793), and also from feminism as an aesthetic movement, marked some two centuries later with the 1929 publication of Virginia Woolf's *A Room of One's Own*. The social strand of feminism concerns itself with women as citizens, and in particular, with their legal rights, whereas the aesthetic strand is more concerned with how women are portrayed in art and literature. Both the social and aesthetic strands share a focus on the examination of the limits placed on women by the societies in which they find themselves, and the extent to which these societies see women as biologically limited rather than as limited by arbitrary, socially constructed conventions. Both strands also form the basis of feminist criticism, which seeks to analyze the total role of women as presented in any given work.

In looking at the part that gender plays in the novels of James Patterson, it is notable that all of the works covered here have strong women characters who carry much of the weight of the narrative (see, for example, *Kiss the Girls* and *Jack & Jill*). However, only *1st to Die* and its sequel, *2nd Chance,* feature women as their primary protagonists, and these are contemporary women who reflect many of the feminist issues of their time. One issue that has been at the heart of the feminist movement is equality of access to professional positions, and all four of these women have positions typically associated with men: police investigator, doctor, lawyer, and journalist. (While it is certainly true that both men and women have traditionally been journalists, it is only recently that women have been able to move from "women's" news beats—society, food, and fashion—to general news, a move that Thomas has made possible for herself by her work on the Honeymoon Murders.)

Another issue of feminism has been the drive to be accepted as an equal outside of the domestic arena, an issue that the protagonist Lindsay Boxer epitomizes when she says she joined the police because "I wanted to prove I could make a difference in a man's world" (118). Closely allied to this is the matter of how women fare in the male world of work outside of the home, particularly in terms of such concepts as the glass ceiling, a term reflecting the fact that women can often go only so high professionally while men with equal qualifications are free to pass beyond them. Boxer articulates this issue when she describes her best friend, Claire Washburn, as a victim of both sexism and racism, saying that Washburn should be head of the Office of Coroner but that her male boss takes the credit for her fine work. "Maybe," Boxer thinks, "the idea of a female M.E. still didn't cut it, even in San Francisco. Female, and black" (48). A similar consciousness of herself as a female trying to succeed in a predominantly male-oriented world, at least in terms of her profession, is always with Boxer and is an underlying motivation for her forming the Women's Murder Club, a group of women who, as Boxer sees them, "would get a kick out of showing up the male orthodoxy" (126). This group is also a fine example of sisterhood, a philosophical concept whose focus is the fact that women, living as they do in a hostile world, should help one another succeed rather than compete with one another for the few places available to them in that world.

As women have become more aware of sexism and its effects on their professional opportunities, they have simultaneously become more sensitive to signs of discrimination against them simply because they are women. Patterson shows this in Boxer's tendency to see sexism everywhere, even in places where motivations are open to question. For example, when a case is taken from her and her partner, her response is "*Goddamn, son-of-a-bitch, controlling men*" (161; italics in original) even though, in this particular situation, her partner is male. She is also specific that it is difficult for her to trust men, perhaps because of the fact that her father abandoned the family when she was thirteen and then she was abandoned again by her husband. These are only hypothetical motivations though, and there is nothing hypothetical about the mistrust. The mistrust is very real and deeply felt by Boxer and it underlines the fact that for most professional women, the consciousness of gender is always with them, whether because of past experiences or present realities.

Patterson's most telling indictment of sexism is reserved not for the actions and reactions of the members of the Women's Murder Club, though, but for the degradation of women by the antagonist, Nicholas Jenks. His first wife says that their marital relationship consisted of his humiliating her. She believes that his second marriage is a repeat of the first, saying that she sees his new wife at various functions and that in her face, "I see the fear. I know how it is. When she looks in the mirror, she no longer recognizes the person she once was" (276). Although the first wife is a beautiful woman, she has apparently formed no new romantic relationships and the profession she has developed for herself since her divorce from Jenks, that of a martial arts instructor, suggests that she has become a woman who never again intends to be vulnerable. The second wife is the tool Jenks uses to commit the murders and these are murders that particularly seek out women since, although they are of male/female couples, it is in every case the woman who is sexually violated after death. Jenks is manipulating a woman to violate other women, and in the context of the novel, this is a believable scenario. Overall, this pattern of a mastermind controlling a series of carefully staged murders performed by a woman emphasizes such feminist issues as the malleability of women in the face of male domination. The fact that both wives, as well as Jenks, end up dead is some small sign of hope that, ultimately, such domination will not succeed, although these deaths do nothing to bring back the murdered couples. At best, the book ends with the message that while the abuse of women can be defeated by brave women acting in concert to do so, it nonetheless causes great harm that cannot be undone.

12

2nd Chance (2002)

2nd Chance is an exception to the other books covered in this Critical Companion in that it is the result of a collaboration between Patterson and the writer Andrew Gross. Throughout this consideration of Patterson's work, I have chosen to write only about the novels that Patterson has written as a single author (he has a total of four novels written with others: 1996's *Miracle on the 17th Green,* with Peter de Jonge, 2002's *The Beach House,* also written with de Jonge, *2nd Chance,* discussed here, and 2003's *The Jester,* written, like *2nd Chance,* with Gross). The single-author novels are Patterson's signature works; these are the novels that have brought him great popular fame, and they are the ones that allow me to focus on Patterson as a writer and craftsman. However, I have made an exception to this single-author rule and included *2nd Chance* here because it is a continuation of what promises to be a new Patterson series, the Women's Murder Club stories, begun with 2001's novel, *1st to Die*. This particular series seems, as of this writing, to be on its way to replacing the Alex Cross novels as Patterson's locus of interest. As to his sharing of the authorship, in an interview with *Seattle Times* critic Diane Wright, Patterson says of working with another writer that this is what he did for a long time in advertising, a field that he describes as "a collaborative process," adding, "Teamwork can work" (2003, E3–4).

GENRE

As is common with Patterson's work, *2nd Chance* combines a number of genres: the girl detective (see Chapter 11 for a fuller discussion of this genre), the classic mystery, with its search for clues that will disclose a murderer and bring him or her to justice, the romance, one of Patterson's favorite genres and one that he includes in some guise in virtually all of his works, and most predominantly, the police procedural, "the subgenre of mystery and detective fiction in which the mystery is solved by the police as part of their professional duties" rather than being solved by a brilliant private detective such as Sherlock Holmes (Kotker 2001, 617). Patterson has used the procedural genre before in his Alex Cross series (see especially *Roses Are Red*). However, *2nd Chance* is one of his most thorough explorations of the procedural, especially in terms of the working relationships within the many different groups that make up a modern police department. The major elements here are the close friendships formed by Lindsay Boxer, the lead homicide detective on this case, Claire Washburn, San Francisco's chief medical examiner, and Jill Bernhardt, an assistant district attorney in the San Francisco prosecutor's office, relationships established in the series novel preceding this, *1st to Die,* and continued in much the same vein in *2nd Chance.*

What is new in *2nd Chance,* though, is the attention paid to the secondary police department personnel and to the everyday working relationships and in-group code words that create a sense of community in any large organization. Thus, someone unnamed from the auto theft division warns Boxer, "Heads up, Lieutenant. Weight's on the floor" (24) and the reader learns that "Weight" refers to the chief of police. There are good specific details on how the crime scene unit team goes about doing its work, information that, without being really necessary to the plot, adds to the sense of police professionalism. The secretary of the division, Karen, warns Boxer that the chief is looking for her and "He sounds mad" (37), establishing the supportive and even protective relationship she feels toward the police she works with. Then there are insider comments that add authenticity to the scenes, as when one detective mentions offhandedly that it is most unusual for a spree killer to switch methods of killing. There are even details on the support provided to the investigation by the personnel department, an integral part of any large group whose inclusion here adds a sense of a realistic organization and its workings to the novel.

Another convention of the police procedural is its attempt to realistically portray the working lives of most police. When Boxer is looking into the background of one of the police officers tied to the victims, she comments that like most cops, he "had one of those proud, uneventful careers, never in trouble, never under review, never in the public's eye" (102)—in other words, policing was his job and he did it in the routine, predictable way that most of us go about doing our jobs, too. Other elements that are standard in procedurals are comments on the long, exhausting hours the police must put in when in the midst of an investigation. They end up short on sleep and short on food, and this is highlighted in Boxer's discussion with a crime scene unit technician who tells her that he's slept at his desk twice in this one week. He wonders, "Doesn't anyone get killed during the day anymore?" (117) as he eats his breakfast of Doritos chips. With the exception of Boxer, Bernhardt, and Washburn, the characters referred to here play minor roles in the resolution of the murders and in the overall plot development. However, they provide an atmosphere that makes of this novel one of Patterson's most complete police procedurals to date.

PLOT DEVELOPMENT

As with all James Patterson books, *2nd Chance* begins with a prologue. A group of African American children, leaving a choir practice, are strafed and one is killed, setting the stage for a killer who at this point seems to be racially motivated. The story line then switches to the Women's Murder Club, continuing the theme established in *1st to Die* and establishing the original situation (see Chapter 3 for discussion on plot analysis), in which Lindsay Boxer, protagonist of these two novels, is on sabbatical leave and is now attempting to put her life back together after the trauma of the Honeymoon Murders and the death of her partner and lover in the first of this series' novels. Complications occur with the death of 11-year-old Tasha Catchings, a little girl attending choir practice. Who would want to kill a small child, and why? Boxer is drawn back to work as the head of the investigation and immediately learns that this may be the second in a planned pattern of killings rather than the random attack it initially appears to be, that the lynching of an elderly African American woman has preceded it. These deaths give all the appearance of being hate crimes, except that evidence left at one of the murder scenes indicates that the killer is also African American, making motivation yet more complex.

The first significant clue adding to complications is the discovery of a gang logo used on a van implicated in the killings, that of a monster from Greek mythology known as a chimera, described by *Webster's New World*

Dictionary as "a fire-breathing monster, represented as having a lion's head, a goat's body and a serpent's tail" (1974, 130). Cindy Thomas, the fourth member of the Women's Murder Club, tells Boxer, "the lion represents courage, the body of the goat stubbornness and will, and the serpent's tail stealth and cunning. It means that whatever you do to crush it, it will always prevail" (96). Boxer, with the help of the club, discovers that this is the symbol of a right-wing hate group, the Templars, and that each of the victims, in addition to being African American, has ties to the San Francisco police department.

Complications continue with a third killing, this time of a police patrolman, followed in short order by the killing of the San Francisco chief of police. Both the patrolman and the chief are African American and at this point it seems clear that the crimes are part of a vendetta against African Americans connected in some way to the San Francisco police department. With the killing of the chief the FBI is brought in, since the crime has now become a federal offense. However, this is an undeveloped plot line, and for all intents and purposes, the mystery remains one that is investigated and solved by the San Francisco homicide department and in particular, by Boxer.

The clue of the chimera is traced to a prison gang at a California prison, and here Boxer learns that the killer may well be a policeman. The next victim is Claire Washburn, the African American medical examiner for San Francisco, who is wounded but not killed, and the trail then leads to Frank Coombs, a one-time policeman charged and convicted many years ago in the unprovoked death of a teenager. Coombs has recently been released from prison and does indeed seem to be seeking vengeance, as Boxer has postulated. However, all James Patterson readers know by now that Coombs must be a red-herring, that in Patterson novels the real murderer is never the most likely suspect, and indeed, despite all the evidence against Coombs, Boxer shows that he cannot be the killer; he has Parkinson's disease and it is impossible that he could be capable of the superb marksmanship that is a signature of this perpetrator. In the climax, the reader discovers that instead of Coombs it is his son, a brilliant Stanford student and athlete, who has carried out the killings. The son's motive was revenge for himself, for his loss of Frank Coombs: "You don't have the slightest idea what it's like to lose your father. You bastards took my father" (375), he tells Boxer, not realizing the irony of his statement given that she, too, has lost a father, although by abandonment rather than imprisonment. Boxer then kills the son in a shoot-out in Hoover Tower on Stanford's campus.

In the denouement or wrapping up of the crime, the major focus is on healing. This is presented in an epilogue in which the church where the little girl was shot is shown restored, Boxer comes to terms with the fact that her father really does love her and, at the same time, is a very poor parent, and the Women's Murder Club is about to get together once again for a Friday night dinner.

CHARACTER DEVELOPMENT

As with *1st to Die,* the main character in *2nd Chance* is its protagonist, Lindsay Boxer, also the protagonist of the first novel. She is the most well-rounded of any of the characters in the book, in that we have information about both her professional life and her personal life. Professionally, she was the first homicide detective in San Francisco and now she is the department's first female lieutenant, a testament to her skill in her field. She has been married and divorced, she has survived a potentially fatal disease as well as the death of her lover, and she is very much a loner, with the exception of her close friendship with the three other women of the Women's Murder Club. She lives by herself, along with her dog Martha, and is still coming to terms with her father's abandonment of the family when she was only 13. Now, at age 35, she would very much like to have a child but feels that she probably won't because, she says, "Parenting just didn't seem like the natural occupation in my family" (62). She is the daughter of a policeman and when she is attacked on a stakeout he is there to rescue her, adding to the ambiguity of his role as a parent. Finally, Boxer is a static character, remaining the same at the end of the novel as she was at the beginning: professionally astute, personally searching. (See Chapter 3 for character analysis details.)

The other major protagonists are Boxer's colleagues and friends, who make up the Women's Murder Club. These, too, were introduced in *1st to Die* and are expanded on here, particularly Jill Bernhardt, the elegant, high-achieving assistant district attorney who has now softened a bit as a result of becoming pregnant. Well into the novel she loses the baby and by novel's end may be pregnant again. Although the reader knows too little about her to see her as dynamic or changing, her wish to have a child is an indication that she is developing as a character from the one-dimensional career woman who was first introduced in this series.

Claire Washburn, who appeared as Boxer's best friend in the previous novel, remains much the same here. She is still, according to Boxer, "the sharpest, brightest, most thorough M.E. the city ever had," (37), and Bernhardt says of her, "She's one of the most capable women I know, at the top of her profession " (58). Claire has the most normal life of the four women; she is happily married, with two children she adores, and as discussed in Chapter 11, she is another example of Patterson's inclusion of positive African American role models in his novels, following such memorable characters as Jimmy Horn in *The Thomas Berryman Number* and Alex Cross, in the many novels covered in this Critical Companion.

Cindy Thomas is the fourth member of the Club. She began her career in this series as a rookie reporter for *The Chronicle* and has now advanced, in *2nd Chance,* to the position of lead crime reporter. She is the only non-law-enforcement member of the Club, and it is she who is the center of the romance sub-plot here, one whose outcome is left open. Although she has certainly advanced in her profession, she is still very much the feisty, independent, excellent researcher introduced in the first Women's Murder Club novel, and so she too is a static character.

Other protagonists consist of various people Boxer works with on this investigation: Chief Mercer, Boxer's superior, Warren Jacobi, Boxer's original homicide partner who now works under her, and Aaron Winslow, a minister who was a chaplain in Desert Storm and is the pastor of LaSalle Heights Church, where the first of the Chimera killings took place. Winslow is a very attractive character, a genuinely good person with little illusions who says of his worldview, "I don't deal in innocence. I've spent too much time in the real world" (78). His parishioners think very highly of him, and like Washburn, he too is an example of Patterson's positive African American characters. Winslow is the other half of the Cindy Thomas romantic sub-plot, and it will be interesting to see how this plays out in future novels in this series, given the interracial nature of the relationship. Patterson has dealt with sociological and racial themes before, most noticeably in the first Alex Cross novel, *Along Came a Spider,* and this new series, with the burgeoning Winslow-Thomas relationship, seems a natural for a continuation of these themes.

Of the antagonists, there are three who play significant roles: Frank Coombs, Weiscz (a character known only by his last name), and Rusty Coombs, Frank's son. While none of these is really a well-rounded character, since we have little information on their formative years, their loves and hates, their dreams and wishes, each is drawn vividly and fully takes up the space allotted to him. Frank Coombs is a street cop who was sent to prison for excessive force, where, according to a prison warden, he "turned into more of a bastard . . . than he was on the outside" (232), choking a cell mate. Frank is the stereotype of the racist policeman, assuming that all African Americans exist outside of the law, and when Coombs is arrested, he is certain that he is a victim of reverse prejudice. He is an excellent candidate for the murderer in this novel except that, as it turns out, he is physically incapable of having done the killings.

The second of the antagonists, Weiscz, is also very well drawn despite the lack of background detail we're given on him. He is an inmate in a maximum security prison, Pelican Bay, having been sent there from Folsom Prison where he was head of an Aryan brotherhood gang and where he strangled an African American guard. His physical description is horrifying: "Strapped to a metal chair, his feet bound in irons, his hands cuffed from behind, hunched a hulking, muscular shape. . . . His hair was long and oily and straggly" (192), and he is covered in tattoos. In a scene that will remind readers of Clarice Starling's first terrifying encounter with Hannibal Lector in the novel *The Silence of the Lambs* (1988), Boxer is warned not to get closer than five feet to Weiscz: "This sonofabitch eats chains," the warden tells her (193). Boxer is visiting Weicz to gain information on Chimera, an Aryan prison gang that he led, and this is really all we know of him. Where and how he grew up, became involved in crime, and ended up in jail are all unknown. However, if he lacks depth, he is certainly convincing as a static character; the reader leaves the scenes with Weiscz certain that any possible change that might take place in this character will only be for the worse—he is indeed a portrait of evil.

The final antagonist is Rusty Coombs, son of Frank, and again, he is a seemingly flat character in that very little information appears to be provided about him. However, on examination, there is actually a good bit of information here; readers are misled because, in reading about the killer, they have no idea that this person will turn out to be Rusty. In his role as the unnamed killer, we learn that he is exceptionally good at video games, he carries a C-l grenade in his pocket as a good luck charm, his motive in the killings is punishment (although not until the end of the novel is it made clear just who is being punished, and for what offense), he is highly skilled with guns, and like all Patterson killers, he has enormous self-confidence and self-esteem. Most frightening is the detail that he has a collection of photographs of lynchings and that these act as erotica for him. In his role as Coombs's 18-year-old son, Rusty is a fine athlete, attending Stanford on an athletic scholarship, and he is obviously also a very intelligent young man, since Stanford is one of the most prestigious universities in the country. According to his mother, he has no relationship with his father and identifies instead with his step-father, and it is this particular piece of misinformation that makes of him a most surprising villain. The reader is astonished to discover that it is Rusty who is the killer and accepts it because it does provide a neat twist to the ending rather than because it is a logical development of what has gone before. Thus, it is difficult to identify Rusty as a round character because although there is a good deal of information on him, only readers who, at the end of the novel, backtrack to discover what details actually apply to him can fill out the portrait. For the average reader, he remains a flat character, Rusty, the 18-year-old student, and he is also static—he does not live long enough for any change to come about.

A final character who lives in a netherworld between protagonist and antagonist is Boxer's father, Marty Boxer. He too was a San Francisco policeman. He abandoned his family when Boxer was 13 and she has never known why. It has now been 10 years since she's seen him and her most vivid recollection of him is that he left Lindsay with the responsibility of taking care of her mother when she was dying. He was apparently a good policeman—at least, other old-timers on the force still remember him and think well of him—although his personal demons affected his ability to maintain his professional commitment, just as they did his personal commitments, and at this point he is working in private security. In *2nd Chance* he makes contact with Boxer because, he says, he wants to make amends. He is a man of great personal charm, so much so that she sees him now as "just a man who had made mistakes . . . no longer someone I could blindly resent" (203).

Marty Boxer moves in with his daughter and it would seem that all is well, that he has come full circle and that she once again has a parent who loves her. Then in a typical Patterson plot switch, it turns out that he himself was involved in the Coombs killing of the teenager all those years ago, the killing that is at the root of today's Chimera murders. It is therefore highly likely that his motive in returning to be with his daughter has little to do with mending fences and a great deal to do with protecting himself from possible retribution from Coombs. This is never absolutely clear, though, since at one point he is responsible for saving Lindsay's life, an action that could have been his intent or could be another attempt on his part to protect himself. Lindsay's final estimate of him is that he is a man who had "conned and bullshitted and disappointed anyone who ever loved him" (307). At the end of the novel he sends her a letter from Mexico, where he is now living on a ramshackle boat named after her. He tells her in this letter that he loves her, and perhaps he does, or perhaps he is storing up points for the next time he needs someone. In this way, he is a flat character, since we know too little about him to understand how he has become the person he is, and he is also static; there is nothing here to indicate that he has, or ever will, change from the charming con-artist he is introduced to us as.

SETTING

As has been noted in earlier chapters, as a general rule setting, both natural and artificial, plays a small part in James Patterson novels, with their strong emphasis on plot. However, he can be a master of setting as a gothic element that contributes fear and dread to his stories. Probably the best example of this is in *Along Came a Spider,* with its descriptions of children buried alive at an abandoned farm. He is also very good at describing the horrors of institutions that are meant to help people and that instead serve to demonstrate society's inability to cope with the mentally ill and the criminal. This skill is apparent as early as Patterson's first novel, 1976's *The Thomas Berryman Number*, where a character is shown in the claustrophobic seclusion room of a mental hospital, a place so bare and cold that the reader needs no convincing that there is something very, very wrong with anyone for whom this constitutes a therapeutic space. Patterson has also created vivid descriptions of death row in *Four Blind Mice*, descriptions that make the sociological comment that we handle all aspects of the death penalty very poorly and that people might well be better off dead than incarcerated for years in a suspended state where they wait to die. Whatever one's stance on the death penalty, one leaves this novel convinced that there has to be a better way, and it is Patterson's use of setting that makes this argument a cogent one.

In *2nd Chance* Patterson returns to the prison scene, this time Pelican Bay Prison, a place, Boxer says, "where the sun don't shine" (188). She adds that this is a prison no law enforcement agent wants to visit, a place where, at the front gate, there is an ominous warning that anyone taken hostage is on his or her own, that there will be no negotiations, suggesting that hostages have indeed been taken here and that it is quite likely they will be taken again. The isolation unit is painted a dull, sterile white and "Monitors and security cameras were everywhere. *Everywhere*" (192). Pelican Bay's warden refers to it as "ground zero of the human race" and mentions that the prisoner Boxer has come to interview was uncooperative and had to be "extracted" from his small cell, a terrifying word-choice here with its connotations of dragging out by the roots. The dehumanization of this site is emphasized when it turns out that the gift Boxer can use to barter for information with the inmate she is visiting is that of a mirror. "Shine it on me," he says. "I haven't seen myself in over a year" (196). This inmate is leader of a prison gang that uses Chimera as its totem and the setting in which he's placed is absolutely convincing in establishing the menace and terror of the group, adding credibility to the horror of the killings taking place outside of the prison.

POINT OF VIEW

In both of the Patterson series considered here, the Alex Cross series and now the Women's Murder Club series, Patterson uses a double point of view as the perspective from which the stories are told: first person for his primary protagonists (Cross and Lindsay Boxer) and third person omniscient for all other characters (see Chapter 3 for a fuller discussion of point of view). When Patterson is writing in first person, the story is told using the "I" voice, a technical device that causes the reader to identify with the narrator. As noted in earlier chapters, this is an intimate voice that blurs the distinction between narrator and reader so that when the narrator is puzzled, so too is the reader; when the narrator is angry, the reader understands the source of the anger; and when the narrator is betrayed, the reader too feels betrayed, having experienced events as the narrator has. This use is particularly effective in *2nd Chance* in the relationship between Boxer and her father; we are able to see, from her perspective, both her well-founded distrust of him and, at the same time, her longing for a parent who loves her. It also works well to show the horrors of the prison system; if Boxer, who is part of the law enforcement establishment and has wide experience with all aspects of it in California, is so appalled by the conditions under which the Chimera leader is held, the reader is even more appalled. Boxer is someone who knows whereof she speaks and her reaction magnifies the reader's reaction, since the reader has already bonded with her perception.

When Patterson shifts to third person omniscient, in which an unidentified omniscient narrator who can see into the minds of all the characters tells the tale, this allows him to introduce a large cast of characters, from the Women's Murder Club to the San Francisco police to Frank Coombs and his son, in a format he has used before, where an all-knowing narrator appears to be sharing full information with the reader but, in actuality, is misleading the reader. We are given just enough detail to create the impression that we know everything important about a character, but in fact, we are missing some significant details and are thus being led astray at the same time that we think we are being informed. A fine example of this is the introduction of the killer playing a video game in an arcade. He is shown as a superb marksman and also as someone who is clearly confrontational—he is the only white person in the game room and, we're told, "that was why he chose to be here" (32). What is left out is any physical description of him that would alert us to the fact that he's an 18-year-old and so the plot line that involves his father as the most likely killer remains throughout the novel as the dominant one in the reader's mind. Of course the whole point of mystery and detective fiction is to mislead the reader up until the last moment, and this use of third person omniscient allows Patterson to effectively do so. Thus, with the mix of the two points of view, readers are able to relate strongly to the protagonist and at the same time be led astray, as all dedicated mystery buffs hope to be.

THEMATIC ISSUES

One strong theme of James Patterson's *2nd Chance* is that it is difficult, if not impossible, to really know another human being. This is apparent in Jill Bernhardt, one of the four members of the Women's Murder Club. She is the epitome of the successful career woman: chic, self-confident, at the top (or as near the top as most women get) of her profession. She is, in this novel, an assistant district attorney, and everyone assumes that when the current district attorney steps down, she will be next in line for the position. Married to an investment banker, Bernhardt surely has it all: looks, money, profession, and marriage. Then we learn that the drive to succeed rules Bernhardt to the point where she cannot let up, that her arms are covered with scars from her high school and college suicide attempts, and that she is a profoundly lonely person, someone who as a child imagined herself as being in a world where everyone else was asleep and she was the only one awake. When the novel opens she is celebrating the fact that she is pregnant, and when she loses the baby, she blames herself: "I just didn't want it badly enough," she tells Boxer (210). Boxer blames the loss of the baby on Bernhardt's husband, although the novel offers no evidence that this is indeed the case. What is to the point is that in many ways, Bernhardt is unknowable; the successful woman she appears to be is very different from the lonely woman she is, although up to this point, only one of her closest friends, Boxer, is aware of this.

Marty Boxer, Lindsay's father, is another example of someone who is ultimately unknowable. He presents himself as a remorseful loser who has backed out of all the responsibilities of his life: his wife, his children, and his profession. Now an older man, he wants to redeem himself and particularly to re-establish relationships with his children, simply, he says, because he loves them. Then it turns out that perhaps the only person he really loves is himself, since his primary motivation in contacting his children seems to be to cover up his past involvement in a killing.

A sadder example of the inability to know another person is Rusty Coombs, the child of Frank Coombs and, in a surprise ending, the killer in *2nd Chance.* Frank Coombs is the first suspect as killer, and when Boxer visits his ex-wife, Rusty's mother, to see if he has contacted the family now that he is out of prison, she tells Boxer that her son has absolutely no contact with his father, that she has always kept them apart and that there are no links between them. When Boxer interviews Rusty he at first assures her that his mother is correct and he says emphatically of Coombs, "He's not my father. . . . My father's name is Theodore Bell. He's the one who brought me up" (253). Matters become a bit less clear-cut, though, when Rusty mentions that he wrote to his father when he was in jail and met with him after he was released. This is definitely not the relationship his mother envisions, one that ends in Rusty's vengeance killing on behalf of his father. Thus, in this novel, friends do not really know friends, children do not really know their fathers, and mothers do not really know their children. Bernhardt's vision of a lonely world in which we are all isolated from one another has much support in *2nd Chance.*

ALTERNATIVE READING: THE FRIENDLY READER

Readers of popular fiction—science fiction, mysteries, romances, Westerns, and the like—have definite expectations of each particular genre. Science fiction, no matter what else it does, must have some scientific concept projected into a different time and developed beyond its actual contemporary practice. A mystery must have some sort of central question and that question must in some way be resolved at the novel's end. A romance must have two people in love who find resolution of their love at the conclusion. A Western must be set in some recognizable Western setting and must consider the importance of the individual as a causative agent.

Readers who choose popular fiction for their entertainment assume that their anticipations regarding a specific genre will be fulfilled, and they are willing to go some good way in cooperating with the author so that this can happen. They are basically friendly readers. They are more than willing to accept that a murder could occur in a locked room, provided the author gives them some reason—and it doesn't have to be all that plausible a reason—to accept this notion. And they are more than willing to accept that there are superior beings on other planets who come from civilizations far in advance of ours and who long to do nothing more than journey to earth and give us their wisdom. All readers ask in return for such acceptance is that the author go half-way with the reader in creating a scenario by which such benevolence on the part of alien races can be accepted, at least for the duration of the story.

Readers are willing to take part in a conspiracy with the author—to pretend that fantasy is reality—because they enjoy the genre or genres involved and because they want to be entertained. The technical term for conspiring with the author in this way is "the willing suspension of disbelief," which is defined as "the willingness [of the reader] to withhold questions about truth, accuracy, or probability in a work. This willingness to suspend doubt makes possible the temporary acceptance of an author's imaginative world" (Holman and Harman 1992, 464).

Every work of fiction ultimately depends on such suspension of disbelief. After all, the reader on some level really does know that the story is only a story and that the characters are only make-believe. Nonetheless, so great is our love of stories and storytelling that we are more than willing to accept the fiction for reality, at least while we are reading the story, if only the author will give us the bare bones of plausibility that will allow us to do this—to enter the world of the author and pretend that it is the real, everyday world.

One interesting way of analyzing a work of fiction—particularly a work of popular fiction, where there are definite audience expectations—is to consider exactly how the author has gone about creating plausibility for the reader. For example, in *2nd Chance,* readers are asked to accept that Lindsay Boxer, a lieutenant in the police department, is a target of the Chimera killer. Now, the plot has established that this killer is seeking vengeance for a policeman being sent to prison some 20 years ago, before Boxer had even finished school. How likely is it that, with no connection to the original situation, she would be on the killer's list? Well, not all that likely, but it does make the killer scarier: he or she isn't afraid to take on a top cop. And because we want to believe that the threat is a real threat, we accept that the killer would do this, despite its lack of fit with his established pattern.

Another excellent example of a writer depending on a friendly audience is the Women's Murder Club. How likely is it that a police lieutenant, a medical examiner, and an assistant district attorney would meet with a reporter after work and outside of a professional setting to discuss an ongoing investigation? Through doing this, all three are risking their jobs and the reporter is risking being given access to any information again. Nonetheless, the reader accepts it because the concept of the Women's Murder Club is fun; it's like children playing in a hidden fort, making pacts with one another, allied against the outside world, and just think, maybe one of us could be included in the group too, if we were loyal enough in our friendships. Patterson also defuses the implausibility of the situation by having the women discuss the fact that they are taking chances in meeting this way and swearing one another to secrecy. "Oh," the reader thinks, "they know that this is dangerous and they've made good preparations to protect themselves." In reality, such meetings are extremely unlikely; in the novel, they work because the reader wants them to, wants, by extension, to be one of the secret gang.

Another highly implausible event is Boxer's going after the killer on her own, given that she has the option of waiting for a back-up SWAT escort. Ah, but the killer is shooting from a tower and could well kill more people while everyone stands around and waits, and so Boxer goes up into the tower all by herself. Would this really happen? Probably not, but readers accept it because heroes are supposed to act in heroic ways and what could be more heroic than acting on one's own to save human lives? And again, Patterson helps the reader to accept the implausibility of the action by having Boxer ask herself, "Why am I doing this?" (367). Ah yes, we think, she recognizes that it is out of the ordinary, so that's okay.

Boxer is the center of other implausible events: the FBI is called in on the case because a federal official has been murdered, but they quietly back out when Boxer comes up with answers and the acting chief decides to go with his local team. Hmmm. Can the FBI be called in and then sent home in quite this casual a way? Well, we'd like to think so because we want this to be Boxer's case—she is the character we identify with, and if she succeeds, so do we, and certainly we have no identification with the faceless FBI agents. Next, Boxer's father follows her on a stake-out, much to her astonishment, and saves her life. Would a skilled police lieutenant, especially one fully alert to her surroundings given that she is on a stake-out, be unaware that she was being followed? It seems unlikely, but readers are so surprised that the follower is Boxer's long-estranged father that they glide over the fact of the unobserved trailing. And what's a father for, if not to save a daughter? Again, would Boxer really have her father move in with her after the years of abandonment and neglect? Well, it adds to the police background of the story (he is a good source of information on the department as it was in the days when Frank Coombs was a policeman), and it's comforting to think that old wounds can be healed and families reunited.

A similar objection applies to the relationship between Rusty Coombs and his father, Frank. Rusty is an only child, adored by a mother who is determined to shield him from his rogue-cop father. Wouldn't she be hyper-alert to any possible effort at contact on the father's part once he was released from prison? And yet, not only has this contact taken place, but Rusty has also been in touch with Frank while Frank was still in prison. Once again, readers accept this because it adds a fine twist to the novel—we absolutely do not expect Rusty to be the villain—and as those of us who have children are all too well aware, parents know far less than they think they do about their offspring. This also raises the question of how believable Rusty is as a killer; he's a very bright athlete, a Stanford student, so how exactly did he become a right-wing fanatic with a hatred of African Americans? Well, this right-wing strand works well to complicate the novel and so readers accept it—we just never know what young people might get up to, and we really do enjoy a multi-string plot.

Another implausibility centered on Rusty is that when he shoots at Claire Washburn, he misses. Hey, wait a minute, he is a superb marksman, something that is reiterated many times in the novel, so how come he missed? She was by herself, highlighted in a window, and was a far better target than some of his previous ones, and yet he missed. Readers want him to miss, though—Claire is a key member of the Women's Murder Club and we want this group to continue so that we can read more of their adventures in subsequent novels and so we think, "Oh well, everybody misses at some time—it could happen."

James Patterson is a master of plotting and quick switches who can always be counted on to give his readers an infrastructure of at least minimal plausibility so that they can become friendly readers, can meet him half-way and make of his novels one best-seller after another. We come to Patterson for thrills rather than authenticity, and without fail, he delivers.

Bibliography

FICTION BY JAMES PATTERSON

Patterson, James. *1st to Die.* Boston: Little, Brown, 2001.
———. *Along Came a Spider.* Boston: Little, Brown, 1993.
———. *Black Market*. New York: Simon & Schuster, 1985.
———. *Cat & Mouse*. Boston: Little, Brown, 1997.
———. *Four Blind Mice*. Boston: Little, Brown, 2002.
———. *Hide and Seek*. Boston: Little, Brown, 1996.
———. *Jack & Jill*. Boston: Little, Brown, 1996.
———. *Kiss the Girls*. Boston: Little, Brown, 1994.
———. *The Lake House*. Boston: Little, Brown, 2003.
———. *The Midnight Club*. Boston: Little, Brown, 1989.
———. *Pop! Goes the Weasel*. Boston: Little, Brown, 1999.
———. *Roses Are Red*. Boston: Little, Brown, 2000.
———. *Season of the Machete*. New York: Ballantine, 1977.
———. *See How They Run*. New York: Warner, 1997.
———. *Suzanne's Diary for Nicholas*. Boston: Little, Brown, 2001.
———. *The Thomas Berryman Number*. Boston: Little, Brown, 1976.
———. *Violets Are Blue*. Boston: Little, Brown, 2001.
———. *Virgin*. New York: McGraw-Hill, 1980.
———. *When the Wind Blows*. Boston: Little, Brown, 1998.
Patterson, James, and Peter de Jonge. *The Beach House*. Boston: Little, Brown, 2002.

———. *Miracle on the 17th Green.* Boston: Little, Brown, 1996.
Patterson, James, and Andrew Gross. *2nd Chance.* Boston: Little, Brown, 2002.
———. *Jester.* Boston: Little, Brown, 2003.

NONFICTION BY JAMES PATTERSON

Patterson, James, and Peter Kim. *The Day America Told the Truth.* New York: Prentice Hall, 1991.
———. *The Second American Revolution.* New York: William Morrow, 1994.

WORKS ABOUT JAMES PATTERSON

Harmon, Melissa Burdick. "Tangents." *Biography,* May 1998: 28.
Hayes, John R. "Along Came Patterson." *Forbes,* 1 Mar. 1993: 128.
"James B. Patterson." *Contemporary Authors on CD.* Gale Group, 2001.
Kellner, Tomas. "Stranger than Fiction." *Forbes,* 10 Oct. 2002: 111–14.
Zaleski, Jeff. "The James Patterson Business." *Publishers Weekly,* 4 Nov. 2002: 43–55.

INTERVIEWS WITH JAMES PATTERSON

Bernard, Andre, and Jeff Zaleski. "Writing Thrillers is Not His Day Job." *Publishers Weekly,* 21 Oct. 1996: 58–59.
Frumkes, Lewis Burke. "A Conversation with James Patterson." *The Writer,* Nov. 2000: 13–14.
"James Patterson: Stop Trying to Write Sentences." *Villagers Interviews.* 17 May 2003 <http://www.ivillage.com/books/intervu/myst/articles/0,,240795_50609,00.html>.
Speidel, Maria. "A Killer at Thrillers." *People,* 20 Mar. 1995: 83–84.
Wright, Diane. "The Prince of the Page Turners." *The Seattle Times,* 10 Mar. 2003: E1.

REVIEWS AND CRITICISM

1st to Die

Miller, Samantha. Rev. of *1st to Die. People,* 16 April 2001: 50.

2nd Chance

Zaleski, Jeff. Rev. of *2nd Chance. Publishers Weekly,* 18 Feb. 2002: 75–76.

Along Came a Spider

Petrakos, Chris. "Amid the Most Macho of Genre." Rev. of *Along Came a Spider. Chicago Tribune Books,* 21 Feb. 1993.

Stasio, Marilyn. Rev. of *Along Came a Spider. New York Times Book Review,* 7 Feb. 1993: 19.

Cat & Mouse

"Discount the Body Count." Rev. of *Cat & Mouse. The Economist,* 13 Dec. 1997: 14–15.

Stasio, Marilyn. Rev. of *Cat & Mouse. New York Times Book Review,* 23 Nov. 1997: 44.

Four Blind Mice

Ayers, Jeff. Rev. of *Four Blind Mice. Library Journal,* 15 Oct. 2002: 95.

Maslin, Janet. "Extending Franchises: Alive! Dead!" Rev. of *Four Blind Mice. New York Times,* 21 Nov. 2002: E9.

Kiss the Girls

Lyons, Gene. "Suspense Accounts Forget Political Plots." Rev. of *Kiss the Girls. Entertainment Weekly,* 20 Jan. 1995: 46–47.

Pop! Goes the Weasel

Steinberg, Sybil. "Forecasts: Fiction." Rev. of *Pop! Goes the Weasel. Publishers Weekly,* 2 Aug. 1999: 69.

Roses Are Red

Karam, Edward. Rev. of *Roses Are Red. People,* 8 Jan. 2001: 41.

Stasio, Marilyn. Rev. of *Roses Are Red. New York Times Book Review,* 10 Dec. 2000: 35.

The Thomas Berryman Number

Cromie, Alice. Rev. of *The Thomas Berryman Number. Booklist,* 1 May 1976: 1322.

Rev. of *The Thomas Berryman Number. Library Journal,* 1 Mar. 1976: 742.

Violets Are Blue

Maslin, Janet. Rev. of *Violets Are Blue. New York Times,* 29 Nov. 2001: E7.

Stankowski, Rebecca House. Rev. of *Violets Are Blue. Library Journal,* 1 Nov. 2001: 133.

OTHER SECONDARY SOURCES

"Across the Nation." *The Seattle Times*, 4 Apr. 2002: A5.

Anderson-Boerger, Patricia. "True Crime." *The Oxford Companion to Crime and Mystery Writing*. Ed. Rosemary Herbert. New York: Oxford UP, 1999. 469.

Bisbee, Dana. "Virgil Tibbs." *The Oxford Companion to Crime and Mystery Writing*. Ed. Rosemary Herbert. New York: Oxford UP, 1999. 462.

Cuddon, J. A. *The Penguin Dictionary of Literary Terms and Literary Theory*. 3rd ed. London: Penguin Books, 1991.

DeMarr, Mary Jean. "True Crime Writing." *The Guide to United States Popular Culture*. Ed. Ray B. Browne and Pat Browne. Bowling Green: Bowling Green UP, 2001. 856–57.

Holman, C. Hugh, and William Harmon. *A Handbook to Literature*. 6th ed. New York: Macmillan, 1992.

Kotker, Joan G. "Police Procedural." *The Guide to United States Popular Culture*. Ed. Ray B. Browne and Pat Browne. Bowling Green: Bowling Green UP, 2001. 617–18.

Lejeune, Anthony. "Club Milieu." *The Oxford Companion to Crime and Mystery Writing*. Ed. Rosemary Herbert. New York: Oxford UP, 1999. 77–78.

Lemon, Leo T. *Approaches to Literature*. New York: Oxford UP, 1969.

Lynn, Steven. *Texts and Contexts*. New York: HarperCollins, 1994.

Mason, Bobbie Ann. *The Girl Sleuth*. U of Georgia P, 1995.

Pike, B. A. "Journalist Sleuths." *The Oxford Companion to Crime and Mystery Writing*. Ed. Rosemary Herbert. New York: Oxford UP, 1999. 244–45.

Poe, Edgar Allan. "The Murders in the Rue Morgue." *Graham's Lady's and Gentleman's Magazine*, April 1841.

Rollin, Lucy. "Nursery Rhymes." *The Oxford Companion to Crime and Mystery Writing*. Ed. Rosemary Herbert. New York: Oxford UP, 1999. 315–16.

Rosenberg, Betty, and Diana Tixier Herald. *Genreflecting*. Englewood, Colo.: Libraries Unlimited, 1991.

Webster's New World Dictionary. Ed. David B. Guralnik. Cleveland, Ohio: William Collins and World Publishing Co., 1974. 130.

Index

Bold page numbers refer to a title's main entry.

About the Author

JOAN G. KOTKER is a member of the English Faculty at Bellevue Community College in Bellevue, Washington. Her essays on popular fiction have been published in the *Encyclopedia of Popular Culture, The Oxford Companion to Crime and Mystery Writing* and *Great Women Mystery Writers* (Greenwood Press, 1994) among others. She is also the author of *Dean Koontz: A Critical Companion* (Greenwood Press, 1996).

Critical Companions to Popular Contemporary Writers
Second Series

Isabel Allende *by Karen Castellucci Cox*

Julia Alvarez *by Silvio Sirias*

Rudolfo A. Anaya *by Margarite Fernandez Olmos*

Maya Angelou *by Mary Jane Lupton*

Ray Bradbury *by Robin Anne Reid*

Revisiting Mary Higgins Clark *by Linda De Roche*

Louise Erdrich *by Lorena L. Stookey*

Ernest J. Gaines *by Karen Carmean*

Gabriel Garca Mrquez *by Rubn Pelayo*

Kaye Gibbons *by Mary Jean DeMarr*

John Irving *by Josie P. Campbell*

Garrison Keillor *by Marcia Songer*

Jamaica Kincaid *by Lizabeth Paravisini-Gebert*

Revisiting Stephen King *by Sharon A. Russell*

Barbara Kingsolver *by Mary Jean DeMarr*

Maxine Hong Kingston *by E. D. Huntley*

Terry McMillan *by Paulette Richards*

Larry McMurtry *by John M. Reilly*

Toni Morrison *by Missy Dehn Kubitschek*

Walter Mosley *by Charles E. Wilson, Jr.*

Gloria Naylor *by Charles E. Wilson, Jr.*

Chaim Potok *by Sanford Sternlicht*

Amy Tan *by E. D. Huntley*

Anne Tyler *by Paul Bail*

Leon Uris *by Kathleen Shine Cain*

Kurt Vonnegut *by Thomas F. Marvin*

Tom Wolfe *by Brian Abel Ragen*

Critical Companions to Popular Contemporary Writers
First Series—*also available on CD-ROM*

V. C. Andrews *by E. D. Huntley*

Tom Clancy *by Helen S. Garson*

Mary Higgins Clark *by Linda C. Pelzer*

Arthur C. Clarke *by Robin Anne Reid*

James Clavell *by Gina Macdonald*

Pat Conroy *by Landon C. Burns*

Robin Cook *by Lorena Laura Stookey*

Michael Crichton *by Elizabeth A. Trembley*

Howard Fast *by Andrew Macdonald*

Ken Follett *by Richard C. Turner*

John Grisham *by Mary Beth Pringle*

James Herriot *by Michael J. Rossi*

Tony Hillerman *by John M. Reilly*

John Jakes *by Mary Ellen Jones*

Stephen King *by Sharon A. Russell*

Dean Koontz *by Joan G. Kotker*

Robert Ludlum *by Gina Macdonald*

Anne McCaffrey *by Robin Roberts*

Colleen McCullough *by Mary Jean DeMarr*

James A. Michener *by Marilyn S. Severson*

Anne Rice *by Jennifer Smith*

Tom Robbins *by Catherine E. Hoyser and Lorena Laura Stookey*

John Saul *by Paul Bail*

Erich Segal *by Linda C. Pelzer*

Gore Vidal *by Susan Baker and Curtis S. Gibson*